Pickleball Made Simple

How Anyone Can Join the Community, Stay Fit, and Master the Game

Blake Foster

RIVANNA HEIGHTS
— MEDIA —

© Copyright Rivanna Heights Media 2024 - All rights reserved.

The content within this book may not be reproduced, duplicated, or transmitted without direct written permission from the author or the publisher.

Under no circumstances will any blame or legal responsibility be held against the publisher or author for any damages, reparation, or monetary loss due to the information contained within this book. Either directly or indirectly. It is crucial to emphasize that you, as the reader, are the ultimate decision-maker and responsible for your choices, actions, and results.

Legal Notice:

This book is copyright-protected. This book is only for personal use. You cannot amend, distribute, sell, use, quote, or paraphrase any part of this book's content without the author's or publisher's consent.

Disclaimer Notice:

Please note the information contained within this document is primarily for educational and entertainment purposes. All effort has been expended to present accurate, up-to-date, and reliable, complete information. No warranties of any kind are declared or implied. Readers acknowledge that the author does not render legal, financial, medical, or professional advice. The content within this book, designed for your education and entertainment, has been derived from various sources. Please consult a licensed professional before attempting any techniques outlined in this book.

By reading this document, the reader agrees that the author is under no circumstances responsible for any losses, direct or indirect, incurred as a result of using the information contained within this document, including, but not limited to, errors, omissions, or inaccuracies.

Contents

Claim Your Free Pickleball Nutrition Guide!	1
Other Books by Rivanna Heights Media	2
Introduction	3
1. Understanding the Basics	5
2. Developing Your Skills	22
3. Advanced Techniques and Strategies	34
4. Physical Fitness and Nutrition	49
5. Mental and Tactical Game	62
6. The Social Aspect of Pickleball	73
7. Equipment Deep Dive	87
8. Beyond the Court	101
Conclusion	113
Appendix A: Detailed Pickleball Rules	115
Appendix B: 30-Minute Drill Sets	119
Appendix C: Exercise Instructions	129
Appendix D: 10-15 Minute Flexibility Session	134
Appendix E: Essential Gear for Your First Pickleball Session	137
Glossary	139
References	146

Claim Your Free Pickleball Nutrition Guide!

To help you get the most out of your pickleball experience, I'm offering a special bonus: a **free Pickleball Nutrition Guide** designed to keep you energized and performing at your best on the court.

Inside this guide, you'll find:

- **Essential Nutritional Tips**: Learn what to eat before, during, and after your games to maximize your energy and recovery.

- **Hydration Strategies**: Ensure you stay hydrated, especially during those long matches.

- **Weekend Meal Plan**: A detailed plan tailored for busy pickleball enthusiasts.

Get your free guide now by clicking or scanning the QR code:

Other Books by Rivanna Heights Media

The Complete Beginner's Guide to Chat GPT: Unlock Practical AI and Master Prompts to Harness the Full Power of ChatGPT in Just 7 Days

by Ryan Harper

Cryptocurrency Investing 101: Understand Bitcoin, Avoid Mistakes, and Make Money Even If You Are An Absolute Beginner Kindle Edition

by Jordan Taylor

Introduction

DID YOU KNOW THAT pickleball, a sport that began as a family backyard pastime, is now one of the fastest-growing sports in America? Every day, people from all walks of life discover the joys of this unique game that blends elements of tennis, badminton, and table tennis into one dynamic, engaging sport. Whether you're a teenager looking for a fun way to stay active or a retiree seeking to keep your reflexes sharp, pickleball has something to offer.

For those new to the sport, pickleball is played on a court similar to badminton, with a net resembling that used in tennis but slightly lower. The paddles used are bigger than those in table tennis but smaller than tennis rackets, and the ball is akin to a wiffle ball, which makes for an intriguing game of pace and strategy. What makes pickleball truly special, however, is its ability to bring people together, fostering a sense of community among players.

The purpose of "Pickleball Made Simple" is to serve as your comprehensive guide through the intricacies and joys of pickleball. Whether you're picking up a paddle for the first time or are an experienced player looking to refine your skills, this book is designed to help you improve your game in just 30 minutes a day, which can be achieved through quick reading sessions or by following the drill sets included in Appendix B. From understanding the basic rules and selecting the right equipment to learning advanced techniques and engaging in strategic play, each page is packed with valuable insights and practical advice.

My journey with pickleball began several years ago when I stumbled upon a community game at a local park. Since then, my enthusiasm for the sport has only grown. I've competed in tournaments, introduced friends to the game, and coached new players, and now, I aim to share this passion with you. My hope is that by sharing my knowledge and experiences, you'll find the same joy and satisfaction in pickleball that I have.

Pickleball is more than just a sport; it's a vibrant community that thrives on fun, fitness, and friendship. Throughout this book, I invite you to connect with local clubs and online groups to share experiences and challenges, further enriching your pickleball journey.

In the following chapters, we will start with the basics of pickleball, advance through skill development, and explore tactical plays that can turn the tide of any game. Each section is designed to build upon the last, ensuring a solid foundation allowing you to play confidently and competitively.

I encourage you to approach this book not just as a reader but as an active participant in your own pickleball adventure. Apply the techniques, join community games, and, most importantly, enjoy every moment on the court.

As we embark on this journey together, I am thrilled to guide you through every serve, volley, and winning shot. Pickleball has transformed many lives, not just bringing better physical health but also joy and lasting friendships. It is my sincere hope that this book will do the same for you. Welcome to the incredible world of pickleball—let's play!

Chapter One

Understanding the Basics

Welcome to your first official step into the engaging world of pickleball! This chapter is designed to lay down the foundation of your pickleball knowledge and skills. Whether you're here to learn the ropes or to refresh your understanding of the core rules that govern this dynamic sport, you're in the right place. At its heart, pickleball is a game of both finesse and strategy and understanding the basic rules is crucial for anyone looking to enjoy the game, whether casually or competitively. As you dive into this chapter, you may encounter some terms that are new to you. Don't worry—these terms will be explained in detail as we progress, so you'll have a solid understanding by the time we're through.

1.1 The Rules of Pickleball

The essence of pickleball is rooted in its simplicity and the quick, lively interactions that games often entail. The game's primary objective is straightforward – to win, you must score 11 points and be at least 2 points ahead of your opponent. This scoring method ensures that games are competitive right until the end, keeping every point crucial and every **rally** exciting.

One fundamental rule of pickleball that might surprise newcomers is that points can only be scored by the serving side. This rule adds a layer of strategy to the game, emphasizing the importance of a strong **serve** and defensive play. However, some games may use **rally scoring**, where a point is awarded after every rally, regardless of which side served.

When serving in singles, the sequence is pivotal; you serve from the right **service court** when your score is even and from the left when your score is odd. The service court is the designated area on each side of the **net** where the serve must land. This alternation continues throughout the game, adding a rhythmic and strategic element to play. The serve must be made diagonally across the **court** to the opponent's service court and, crucially, without stepping on the **baseline**. This diagonal element not only makes the serve more challenging but also opens up the court, setting the stage for strategic plays. In **doubles**, both partners on a team serve on each turn.

Another fundamental aspect of pickleball is the player's responsibility for making prompt "out" calls on their side of the net, even in matches with a referee. This emphasizes the importance of sportsmanship and honesty in the game. According to the rules, any ball that lands on the line is considered "in," so players must be careful when making these calls. If there is any doubt about whether the ball is "in" or "out," the benefit of the doubt should be given to the opponent. Additionally, players are responsible for calling faults, such as foot faults in the non-volley zone or stepping on the baseline during a serve. Failure to make these calls promptly can lead to disputes, so maintaining clear communication is crucial for a smooth and fair match.

Faults in pickleball are any action that stops play because of a rule violation and act as critical turning points in the game. Unlike tennis, faults can occur on any hit, not just the serve. Common faults include the ball hitting outside the designated play area, failing to clear the net, or violating the **two-bounce rule**. The two-bounce rule mandates that the ball must bounce once on each side before **volleys** are allowed. A volley is a shot taken before the ball bounces, and this rule adds tactical depth to the game. Understanding and anticipating these faults play a significant role in both your defensive and offensive strategies.

The **non-volley zone**, commonly called **'the kitchen,'** is a **zone** on the court extending 7 feet from the net on both sides. No volleying is allowed in this zone, meaning you cannot hit the ball before it bounces while standing in this area. Any ball landing on the kitchen line is considered to be in the kitchen. The purpose of this rule is to prevent players from executing smashes from a position too close to the net, which would unfairly disadvantage the receiving player. The kitchen rule encourages a more tactical game where positioning and shot placement are key. Furthermore, any volley involving the kitchen, either by stepping into it during or after the volley, is a fault. Additionally, both feet must be fully grounded outside the zone when exiting the kitchen before you can volley again. This prevents players from exploiting quick movements to volley immediately after leaving the kitchen.

Here is a summary of the basic rules to get you started quickly:

1. Every rally begins with a serve
2. The correct score must be called before serving
3. The rally continues until a fault occurs
4. You can only score points on your serve
5. The ball must bounce on both sides before either team can volley
6. There is no volleying in the kitchen
7. The first team to 11 points wins-but they must be up by 2

Rule 1: Every Rally Begins with a Serve: Each game and rally begins with a serve in pickleball. The serving player, positioned on the right side of the court, initiates the serve. The serve is directed diagonally across the net to the opponent's court:

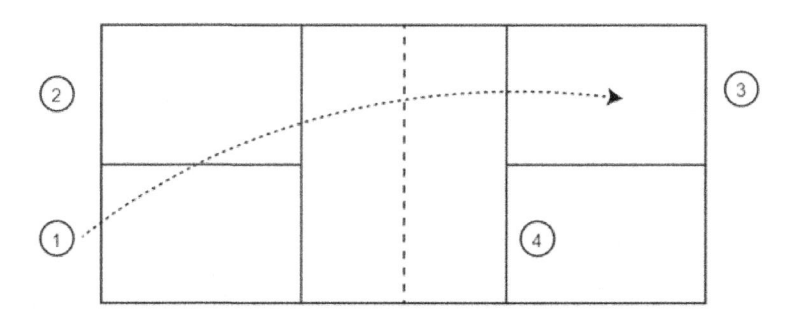

The server can strike the ball after it bounces, known as a **drop serve**, or hit a **volley serve** directly from the air. Regardless of the type of serve, it must clear the kitchen, including its boundary line. For a volley serve, players must execute an underhand stroke using either a

forehand or **backhand** grip, making contact with the ball below waist level. Additionally, the **paddle** must follow an upward arc during the striking motion.

Rule 2: The Correct Score Must be Called Before Serving: In pickleball, players must announce three numbers in doubles, such as '0-0-1', and two numbers, such as '0-0' in **singles**. Each number provides specific information:

First Number:	**Second Number:**	**Third Number:**
The score of the serving team	The score of the receiving team	The player who is serving (in doubles)

For example, if the score is 4-3 in a doubles match and you are beginning your serve, you would announce '4-3-1', indicating that you are the first server in the current rotation. If you lose the rally, the ball does not go to the opponents; instead, it is passed to your partner, who will then announce '4-3-2.' If your partner also loses their serve, a **side out** occurs. This means you have used up your team's two serves, and the opponents will now take their turn to serve. The opponents will announce '3-4-1' before starting their serve. The one exception to this rule is at the beginning of a new game when the first server announces '0-0-2'. This is because the starting team only gets a single serve, to begin with, and they have the advantage of being the first to potentially score points in the **match**.

Rule 3: The Rally Continues Until a Fault Occurs: Once the serve is made, play continues until the rally is won, either by hitting a winning shot or when a 'fault' occurs, which ends the rally. In pickleball, there are four common types of faults:

- The serve lands outside the designated **service area** or within the kitchen (including the line)

- The ball lands out of bounds, either beyond the baseline or outside the **sideline**.

- The ball hits the net and stays on your side.

- The ball bounces twice on one side before the player has a chance to return it.

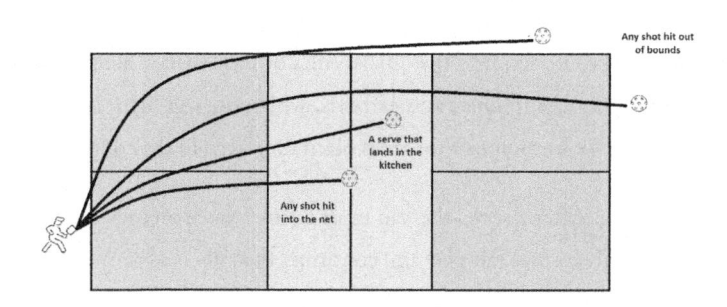

Rule 4: You Can Only Score Points on Your Serve: In typical pickleball scoring, points can only be won while serving, and you continue to serve until your rally is lost. After each successful point on your serve, you and your partner switch sides (left and right), and the serve is directed to the other opponent. If your team loses a point, your partner takes over serving, following the same sequence as before, until your team loses another point. The serve sides out at that point, meaning it passes to the opposing team.

Rule 5: The Ball Must Bounce On Both Sides Before Either Team Can Volley: After the serve, the ball must bounce once on each side of the net before either team can volley (hit the ball in the air without letting it bounce). This means that after the serve, the receiving team must let the ball bounce before returning it, and then the serving team must also let the ball bounce before making their next shot. Only after these two bounces can the ball be volleyed by either team. This is known as the Two-Bounce Rule.

Rule 6: There Is No Volleying In The Kitchen: The 7-foot area on either side of the net designates the kitchen, which is the area where you cannot hit a volley while any part of your body is inside or touching the line. Additionally, your momentum cannot carry you into the kitchen after making a volley. You are, however, allowed to hit the ball after it bounces in the kitchen. If your opponent plays a short shot that lands in the kitchen, you may enter the zone and play the ball from within the kitchen.

Rule 7: The First Team To 11 Wins-But They Must Be Up By 2: Following the rules outlined above, the game continues until one team reaches 11 points, but they must win by a margin of 2 points. So, if the score is tied at 10-10, the game doesn't end with the next point. Play continues beyond 11-10 until one team secures a 2-point lead. As a result, some games can extend for quite a while, with final scores like 12-10, 15-13, or even 21-19.

Six Often Forgotten Rules

It can be confusing to understand the official rules of pickleball. There are also obscure rules, like prohibiting headphones and earbuds, which doesn't help. Let's start from a high-level view and look at some of the rules often forgotten in the court.

Two-Bounce Rule: After a serve, the ball must bounce once on each side before it can be hit in the air. This ensures fair play and continues the rally.

Baseline Serving: Always serve from behind the baseline with at least one foot behind it and no foot touching the line. The ball must be hit below your waist, diagonally across the net.

Non-Volley Zone Restrictions: No volleys are allowed in the kitchen to prevent players from gaining an unfair advantage. Serves can't land in this zone, either. After a volley, you cannot step into the kitchen, and when exiting, both feet must be fully grounded outside the kitchen before volleying again.

Drop Serve: Fully incorporated by USA Pickleball in 2022, the drop serve allows the ball to be dropped from any height and hit after it bounces, offering a different serving option.

10-Second Rule: Servers have 10 seconds from the score call to make their serve. This keeps the game moving and maintains fairness.

Extra Ball Rule: Players can carry an extra ball during play, such as in a pocket, but dropping it during play results in a fault.

Reflective Moment

Take a moment to reflect on these rules. How do they compare to other racket sports you know? Understanding these distinct rules is your first step in not just playing but excelling at pickleball, as each regulation introduces unique challenges and opportunities. Consider how these rules might influence your approach to the game, both as a server and a receiver, and think about strategies you might employ to turn these rules to your advantage. Engage with these reflections actively; jot down thoughts or discuss them with fellow pickleball enthusiasts. This active engagement will deepen your understanding and enhance your play.

By grasping these foundational rules, you are well on your way to not just participating in pickleball but truly enjoying the strategic depth that makes this sport uniquely captivating and enjoyable. As you continue to build upon this knowledge, keep in mind that each rule and regulation is designed to create a balanced, competitive, and fun environment for all players involved.

Please refer to Appendix A for a more comprehensive list of pickleball rules.

1.2 Choosing Your Gear

Selecting the right equipment in pickleball isn't just about having the best tools; it's about finding the gear that complements your playing style, enhances your comfort, and ultimately improves your game experience. When it comes to paddles, there's a surprising variety to choose from, each made from different materials and designed with specific features that cater to various needs. Wood, graphite, and composite paddles each offer unique benefits. Wooden paddles are generally the most affordable and are quite durable, making them a fantastic choice for beginners or schools and community centers. However, they tend to be heavier, which might slow down your reaction time on the court. Graphite paddles, on the other hand, are lighter and offer a stiffer surface, which allows for more precise shot control—ideal for players looking to improve their game precision. Composite paddles are a popular middle-ground option, offering a good balance of power and control with a variety of surface textures to enhance ball spin.

The weight of the paddle and the **grip** size are equally crucial. A heavier paddle can **drive** the ball more powerfully, which might be appealing to those who prioritize strength in their game. However, a lighter paddle enhances maneuverability and reduces the risk of fatigue or injury, which is particularly beneficial for players with joint concerns or those who play frequently. The grip size should comfortably fit in your hand, allowing a natural and firm hold without straining. Remember, playing with a grip too large or too small can lead to discomfort or even injury over time, so it's worth getting this right. There

Paddle Fitting Quizzes

are several online paddle-fitting quizzes to help you find your perfect paddle. Just click or scan the QR code above for a list!

Turning our attention to pickleball balls, we see that the difference between indoor and outdoor balls can impact your play significantly. Indoor balls are typically softer and have larger holes. This design allows them to move slower and less erratically, adapting well to the smoother and more controlled environment of indoor courts. Outdoor balls, made to withstand rougher, more varied surfaces, are more rigid and have smaller, more tightly spaced holes. These features help the ball achieve a more consistent flight path in the breezy conditions you might encounter outdoors. Choosing the right ball depending on where you play most often can drastically affect your ability to control and enjoy the game.

Proper footwear and apparel also play a pivotal role in your pickleball experience. Shoes designed for court sports like tennis or volleyball are ideal for pickleball. They offer the necessary lateral support to handle quick side-to-side movements and have soles that grip the court well, which can prevent slips and falls. Clothing should be lightweight and breathable to keep you comfortable during play. It's also wise to consider moisture-wicking fabrics that can help keep you dry and focused on your game.

Lastly, don't overlook the importance of accessories. Comfort-enhancing grips can help absorb sweat and prevent your paddle from slipping during an intense rally. Sweatbands and protective eyewear are not just about comfort and safety; they also ensure that you can play your best game without distractions. Sweatbands keep sweat away from your eyes and hands, while quality sports eyewear shields your eyes from the sun and stray balls. Protective eyewear is particularly crucial for every player, especially in the early stages when positioning and reflexes are still developing. It's surprisingly easy to accidentally get hit by a ball, a paddle, or even your partner's movement on the court. This simple yet vital piece of equipment ensures that your vision remains sharp and safe, allowing you to fully enjoy and focus on your game.

By thoughtfully selecting each piece of your gear—from your paddle to your shoes—you set yourself up not just for success in pickleball but for a more enjoyable and rewarding experience on the court. Each piece of equipment offers an opportunity to enhance your game, ensuring every serve, volley, and return is as good as possible. Whether you are just starting out or looking to elevate your game, the right gear can make all the difference. Remember, in a sport where every point counts, the details matter just as much.

When purchasing pickleball gear, there are several sources to consider, each offering its own advantages. Local sporting goods stores often carry a selection of paddles, balls, and other accessories, allowing you to physically examine and test different options before making a purchase. For a wider variety and potentially better deals, online retailers like Amazon, Dick's Sporting Goods, and specialty pickleball websites provide extensive selections and customer reviews to guide your choice. Additionally, visiting a dedicated pickleball shop in your area, if available, can offer expert advice and personalized recommendations. Don't forget to check out community centers and pickleball clubs, which sometimes sell gear or can point you toward trusted suppliers. By exploring these various sources, you can find quality gear that suits your playing style and budget, ensuring you are well-equipped to enjoy the game to the fullest.

1.3 The Court Layout

Understanding the layout of a pickleball court is like learning the stage on which the drama of each game unfolds. Each line, zone, and measurement has a role to play in how the game is played, influencing strategies and outcomes. A standard pickleball court is a rectangle measuring 20 feet in width and 44 feet in length, including lines. The net splits the court into two equal halves and is hung at 36 inches on the sidelines and dips to 34 inches in the center. This slight dip in the middle offers a tantalizing challenge: it's an inviting spot for a winning shot but requires skill to target effectively.

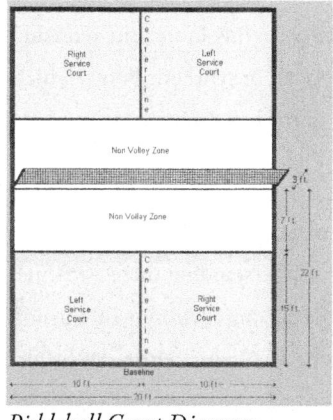

Pickleball Court Diagram

The court is divided into several distinct areas, each with its strategic importance. The service areas are where players serve the ball, and these are located at the back of the court on both sides. Each player or team has two service areas, one on the right and one on the left, and players must serve diagonally across the court to the opposite service area. This requirement for diagonal serving introduces a natural angle into play, opening up the court and making each serve both a challenge to execute and an opportunity to outmaneuver the opponent.

One of the most critical areas on a pickleball court is the non-volley zone, commonly known as 'the kitchen.' This area extends 7 feet from the net on either side, creating a space where the ball must bounce once before it can be hit. This rule prevents players from executing smashes right at the net, a move that makes returning the ball almost impossible and slows down the game's pace. The kitchen is a place where thoughtful strategy and careful control can turn the tide of a game, demanding a blend of precision and patience from each player.

Boundary lines are significant, not just for determining whether a ball is in or out, but also for influencing players' movements and strategies. These lines help define the playing area, and any ball that lands *outside* these lines is considered out of bounds. However, the ball can cross these lines in the air during play, and as long as it lands within bounds, it remains in play. Players often use the full extent of the court, maneuvering their opponents side to side and back and forth, trying to exploit open spaces or create them by drawing opponents out of position.

The orientation of the court can also have a subtle but significant effect on play. For instance, if one end of the court faces directly into the sun, the player on that side will be disadvantaged during sunny conditions. Therefore, many players prefer to choose sides based on the sun's position at the beginning of play, specifically in outdoor settings. Similarly, the type of surface can affect how the game is played. Courts can be made from various materials, including concrete, asphalt, and specially designed modular surfaces. Each material has different characteristics; for example, concrete provides a fast, hard surface that leads to a quicker game, while asphalt can offer slightly more grip, reducing the risk of slips and falls. Indoor courts often feature wooden or synthetic floors, which can be easier on the joints but might change the bounce of the ball compared to outdoor surfaces.

Every detail of the court, from the measurements and materials to the orientation and surface type, plays a role in how pickleball is played. By understanding these elements, players can develop strategies that take full advantage of the playing environment, turning the court itself into a tool for victory. Whether it's using the lower center net height to attempt a risky shot, playing to the boundaries to stretch the opponent's defense, or mastering the unique bounce characteristics of different surfaces, knowledge of the court's layout empowers players to play smarter and more effectively. As you continue to engage with the sport, take the time to familiarize yourself with these aspects of the court. Notice how different surfaces affect your play, practice serving accurately within the confines of the service areas, and always be aware of the sun's position during outdoor games. With this knowledge, you step onto the court, prepared to play and compete.

1.4 The Scoring System

Let's now dive deeper into pickleball scoring to gain a solid understanding. The scoring system in pickleball is straightforward yet distinct, combining elements from both tennis and badminton. Points are only scored by the serving team, and to win, you need to score 11 points and lead by at least 2 points. If the score ties at 10-10, play continues until one side gains a two-point advantage. This aspect keeps competitive games close to the very end, as each side vies to gain and maintain the lead. Some tournament games might be played to 15 or 21 points, but the requirement is always to win by a 2-point margin.

The Serve and Scoring

1. **Serving Sequence**: The game begins with a coin toss or rally to determine which team serves first. The player on the right side of the serving team serves diagonally to the opponent's service court. The serve must clear the non-volley zone (the kitchen) and land in the opposite diagonal court. Additionally, the server must adhere to specific rules to avoid faults. These include keeping their feet behind the baseline until after the ball is struck, not contacting the ball above their waist, and ensuring the ball is struck with an underhand motion. If the server steps on or over the baseline onto the court at ball contact, or fails to make a legal serve, it results in a fault. In doubles, this leads to a loss of serve for that player, passing the serve to their partner or to the opposing team if it is the second server's turn.

    Serving Sequence

2. **Scoring Points**: Only the serving team can score points. If the serving team wins a rally, they score a point, and the same server serves again from the opposite service court.

3. **Faults and Service Loss**: If the serving team commits a fault (such as hitting the ball out of bounds, into the net, or failing to clear the non-volley zone), they lose

the serve. In doubles play, both players on the serving team get a chance to serve before the serve is handed over to the opponents. Except for the initial serve, the serve moves to the second server after the starting server commits a fault.

Doubles Scoring

In doubles, each team has two servers per service turn. The initial serve of the game is an exception where only one server gets to serve. Here's how the scoring sequence works:

1. **Starting the Game**: At the beginning of each game, the serving team starts with only one server, often called "the starting server." This is to balance the serving advantage.

2. **Rotation**: After the first fault, the serve passes to the opponents (side out), who then get their two serves. After both players on the team have served and committed faults, the serve goes back to the original serving team.

3. **Player Positions**: Players switch positions only after scoring a point. The first server always serves from the right-hand side at the start of their team's service turn. After each point won, the server alternates sides with their partner.

4. **Calling the Score**: The score is called in three numbers: the serving team's score, the receiving team's score, and the server number (either 1 or 2). For example, a score of "5-3-1" means the serving team has 5 points, the receiving team has 3 points, and it is the first server's turn.

Singles Scoring

Singles scoring in pickleball follows similar principles but is simpler since each player serves from their side:

1. **Service Rotation**: The player serves from the right service court when their score is even and from the left service court when it is odd.

2. **Scorekeeping**: The score is called with just the server's score followed by the receiver's score. For example, if the server has 7 points and the receiver has 5 points, the score is called as "7-5."

Winning the Game

As mentioned, a game is won when a team or player reaches the required winning score (usually 11, but sometimes 15 or 21 points in tournament play) and is ahead by at least 2 points. If the score reaches a tie near the end of the game (such as 10-10 in an 11-point game), play continues until one side achieves a 2-point lead.

Understanding the scoring system is crucial for both competitive and recreational play. It ensures the game flows smoothly and helps players strategize effectively, knowing when they can score and when they need to focus on regaining the serve.

1.5 Basic Techniques: Serving, Volleying, and Returning

Serving in pickleball, much like in many racket sports, sets the tone for each point, but its unique rules can turn it into a strategic advantage if executed well. The basic serve in pickleball is an underhand stroke, hit below your waist in an upward arc with the paddleface below your wrist. Your stance is crucial here; standing sideways relative to the net can increase your range of motion and control. Position your feet shoulder-width apart, with your paddle hand in front and the hand holding the ball extended out towards the net. This stance not only prepares you for a stable serve but also positions you to move quickly into a ready stance for the return. Aim to hit the ball with a smooth, upward swing when performing the serve, allowing the paddle to follow through naturally. The point of contact is critical — striking the ball too high or too low can lead to faults or ineffective serves.

Four Basic Serves

There are four basic serves in pickleball. The most basic serve, the **Get It In Serve**, is focused on just getting the ball in play. Start with the paddle low and finish high, using this serve until you can consistently get the ball in play. The next serve, the **Lob Serve**, entails following through the ball higher than the Get It In Serve, trying to hit the ball harder and deeper into your opponent's court. The third serve is a **Power Serve**, which involves using your torso to twist while using a lifting motion in your stroke. The Power Serve puts more pressure on your opponent but can be risky, especially for beginners. The fourth serve is the **Angle Serve**, aimed just past the kitchen, angling out of bounds. This is a more difficult serving technique for intermediate to advanced players.

Strategically, where you place your serve can significantly affect the flow of the game. Serving deep into the opponent's court can push them back, limiting their ability to hit a powerful return. Alternatively, varying your serve between short and long can keep your opponent guessing, disrupting their rhythm. If you notice a weakness in your opponent's return shots, you can also address that weakness. These strategic placements require practice, but the payoff in controlling the game's pace is well worth the effort.

The fundamental strokes in pickleball—forehand, backhand, and transitional strokes like the **dink**—are crucial for a well-rounded game. The forehand and backhand are 'drives' and are your primary tools for most shots. For a solid forehand, rotate your body to your dominant side and swing the paddle across your body, finishing with the paddle over your opposite shoulder. For the backhand, it's a similar motion in reverse, with less body rotation. Both shots require a firm wrist and a controlled swing to maintain accuracy and power. The dink, a softer shot aimed just over the net into the kitchen, is a strategic stroke used to pull opponents forward into the court, setting up more aggressive plays. It requires finesse and precision, as the goal is to make the ball land softly in the opponent's kitchen, making it difficult for them to return with power.

Basic Strokes

Moving on to volleys, a volley in pickleball is a shot made in the air before the ball bounces. Given that this must be done outside the non-volley zone or 'the kitchen,' positioning and timing are critical. Effective volleying is about quick reflexes and sharp hand-eye coordination. When you're defending and ready to volley, keep your paddle in front of you and above the net's height with your knees slightly bent. This position ensures you can react quickly to your opponent's shots. The tactical advantage of a good volley lies in its ability to keep your opponent off balance. You shorten your opponent's reaction time by volleying, leading to forced errors or weaker returns that you can exploit.

Beyond volleys, drives, and dinks, several other shots can help you round out your pickleball game. **Drop shots** are crucial for keeping your opponents on their toes, especially when executed from the back of the court to land precisely in their kitchen. **Lobs** can be highly effective for pushing opponents back from the net, giving you time to reposition.

Overheads are powerful tools for attacking lobs before they bounce, often catching your opponents off guard.

The image below highlights the primary pickleball shots, providing a quick reference to their purpose and execution. Mastering these will give you a well-rounded skill set and a strategic advantage on the court.

Drive:	Drop Shot:	Dink:
strong shots that are typically executed after the ball bounces, often from the baseline, using either a forehand or backhand swing.	shots executed from the back of the court designed to land in the opponent's kitchen, preventing them from launching an offensive attack	similar to a drop shot but executed closer to the net, dinks are soft shots aimed into your opponent's kitchen to prevent them from attacking
Lob:	**Overhead:**	**Volley:**
shots that are lofted high into the air to push opponents back from the kitchen	shots struck overhead with a tennis-like serving motion, used to attack lobs before they hit the ground	shots that are struck out of the air before the ball bounces that can only be executed outside the kitchen

These basic techniques form the foundation of effective pickleball play. Mastery of these can significantly elevate your game, turning routine exchanges into strategic, controlled points. Practice these regularly, integrate them into your playing style, and watch as your game transforms, not just in skill level but in your strategic approach to each match.

1.6 Essential Pickleball Terminology

Jumping into the language of pickleball is not just about understanding the rules—it's about immersing yourself in the culture and camaraderie surrounding this vibrant sport. Familiarity with pickleball terminology will enhance your comprehension of the game and enrich your conversations with fellow players, whether you're discussing a recent match or sharing tips. Let's start with some basic terms that form the backbone of pickleball conversations.

First, a **rally** is the exchange of shots between players that begins with the serve and continues until a fault is made. Rallies are the heart of pickleball, where points are fought for, and strategy comes to life. Next, a **fault** is a violation of the playing rules. Common faults include hitting the ball out of bounds, not clearing the net, and volleying from within the kitchen. Understanding faults is crucial as they determine whether points are won or lost.

Two pickleball shots you'll often hear about are the **dink** and the **lob**. A dink is a soft, controlled shot that barely clears the net and lands in the opponent's kitchen. This shot is all about finesse and placement, forcing the opponent to move forward and hit upwards, potentially opening up their court for your next shot. In contrast, a lob is a shot that sends the ball high, sometimes over the opponent's head, ideally landing near the baseline. It's a strategic move to push the opponent back to the baseline, disrupting their positioning and taking them out of an aggressive stance near the net.

Another explosive shot is a **smash**. This refers to a powerful overhead shot, usually hit with a lot of force, aimed at returning the ball to the opponent's court as quickly as possible. Smashes are thrilling to execute and can be literally and metaphorically game-changers. A **drop shot** is a delicate and strategic shot executed from the back of the court, designed to land softly in the opponent's kitchen. The aim is to force your opponent to move forward quickly, making it difficult for them to return the ball with an aggressive shot. Additionally, the serving team commonly uses the drop shot as the third shot to neutralize their opponents' advantage and give the serving team time to advance to the kitchen.

An **overhead** is a powerful shot struck above the head, similar to a tennis serve. It's typically used to attack high lobs, aiming to return the ball to the opponent's court with speed and precision before it bounces. A **volley** is a shot taken out of the air before the ball bounces, usually performed close to the net. Volleys must be executed outside the kitchen in pickleball, as hitting a volley from within this zone is prohibited.

Moving on to the colorful slang that peppers the pickleball community, terms like kitchen, pickle, and banger add a fun twist to the game's lingo. As we have discussed, the **kitchen** refers to the non-volley zone, a key area on the court where volleying is prohibited until the ball bounces. The term itself is thought to come from the phrase "kitchen sink," implying that everything but the kitchen sink could cross the line, just not players attempting a volley.

Pickle in pickleball is often humorously claimed to come from the name of a dog that belonged to one of the sport's inventors, who would chase after errant balls. However, it's more likely derived from the term 'pickle boat,' referring to the last boat to return with its catch in rowing, which metaphorically aligns with the makeshift, scavenged equipment the game was first played with. And whatever you do, don't get **pickled**—a term that refers to losing a game 11-0.

A **banger** is a player who predominantly relies on powerful, hard-hitting shots. "Bang away," the term suggests, often at the expense of strategic play, which can make games with or against bangers quite the adrenaline rush.

Regarding scoring, terms like side out and point on serve are often heard. A **side out** occurs when the ball is served by one team, but the opposite team wins the rally, causing a change in serve possession. This term is crucial because, in pickleball, only the serving team can score points, which makes gaining the service a key tactical objective. **Point on serve** refers to a point scored by the serving team during their service turn, underlining the advantage of holding the serve.

Lastly, **court speak** involves the language players use during matches, including verbal and non-verbal cues. Players often call out "yours" or "mine" to avoid collisions and clarify who will take the shot. Communicating effectively during games is not just about courtesy; it's a strategic element that can significantly enhance teamwork, especially in doubles play.

This is not a comprehensive list of all pickleball terms, but it's a good foundation to feel at home on the court. Understanding these terms and their applications within the game provides a richer, more connected experience in the world of pickleball. Each term is a thread in the larger fabric of pickleball culture, linking players with a shared language that promotes competitive play and community bonding. As you step onto the court, keep these terms in mind. They will help you navigate the game more effectively and deepen your appreciation for the sport and its unique culture. Remember, every sport has its language, and mastering it is just as important as mastering the physical skills.

Chapter Two
Developing Your Skills

As you progress in your pickleball adventure, mastering foundational skills is akin to building a strong, resilient bridge that carries you confidently over challenging waters. This chapter is dedicated to deepening your understanding and proficiency in essential pickleball techniques, starting with one of the most pivotal aspects of the game: the serve. A robust serve sets the stage for what follows; it can be a strategic tool that shifts the dynamics of the game in your favor. Let's dive into how you can transform your serve from a mere starting stroke to a formidable part of your pickleball arsenal.

2.1 Mastering the Serve: Techniques and Practice Drills

The serve in pickleball, while fundamental, holds layers of complexity and strategic depth that can significantly influence the flow of the game. It is the only time in a match where you have complete control over the ball, and thus, it presents a unique opportunity to set up the point in your favor. The most basic serve, the Get It In serve, has several variants. The first variant of the serve we'll explore is the Lob Serve, a high soft serve. This serve is arced high into the air, landing deep in the opponent's court. The intention here is twofold: to give yourself enough time to position yourself optimally after the serve and to push your opponent back, limiting their offensive options. It's particularly effective in windy conditions where the ball's trajectory can be unpredictable and harder to handle.

Conversely, the Power Serve is all about speed and force, driving the ball fast and low over the net to the back of the opponent's court. This serve is designed to rush your opponent, giving them little time to react and potentially forcing a weak return that sets up an advantageous situation for you. Choosing between a high soft serve and a powerful one often depends on your opponent's weaknesses and your comfort with each serving style. Some players find a rhythm in power, while others thrive in the tactical patience required for a softer serve.

The effectiveness of your serve, regardless of the type, heavily relies on your position and body alignment. Proper positioning is crucial; you should stand with your feet shoulder-width apart, parallel to the baseline, with your weight balanced slightly on the balls of your feet. This stance ensures stability and agility, allowing you to move swiftly into an optimal position once the ball is in play. When executing the serve, align your paddle arm's shoulder towards the target, rotate your hips, and shift your weight from the back foot to the front foot as you swing. This body alignment maximizes the power generated from your core, transferring it through your arm and into the paddle, lending force and accuracy to the serve.

Practice Drills for Perfecting Your Serve

To enhance the precision and consistency of your serves, consider setting up targets in different zones of the service box during practice sessions. Use cones or markers to divide the service box into sections and aim to hit each target with both high soft serves and power serves. To simulate match conditions, begin by serving from a stationary position and gradually incorporate movement, serving after a light jog to the baseline. This drill not only improves your accuracy but also your ability to serve effectively under physical stress.

One common mistake beginners make is committing **foot faults** by stepping on the baseline before striking the ball. To correct this, practice serving behind a line drawn a couple of inches behind the baseline. This adjustment trains your muscle memory to respect the boundaries naturally during gameplay. Another frequent error is hitting the serve too high, making it easy for opponents to return aggressively. To remedy this, focus on controlling your paddle's angle and the force of your swing during practice, making adjustments based on where the ball lands.

By dedicating time to practice and refining your serving techniques, you empower yourself to start each point confidently. Whether you choose the strategic placement of a Lob Serve or the assertive pressure of a Power Serve, mastering this aspect of pickleball can provide you with a significant advantage on the court. Remember, every great serve you learn and every mistake you correct builds your competence and confidence, making you not just a player but a formidable competitor in the vibrant world of pickleball.

2.2 Returning the Serve: Strategies to Start Strong

Returning a serve in pickleball can be just as strategic as serving itself, transforming what might seem like a defensive move into an opportunity to gain the upper hand. The key to a strong return lies not only in your physical execution but also in your tactical approach. Let's begin with your positioning on the court, which is fundamental to effectively responding to any serve. Ideally, you want to position yourself in a neutral spot within the baseline area, giving yourself enough room to move in any direction. This stance ensures you can cover the most ground possible without committing too early to any side of the court. Keeping your knees bent slightly and your paddle ready at chest height allows for quick reactions, whether the serve is fast and low or high and deep. Watching the server's paddle and body orientation can give you clues about the likely trajectory of the serve, enabling you to adjust your position preemptively.

When it comes to return techniques, the type of serve you're facing will dictate your response. If you're dealing with a soft serve, the goal is to use a controlled, smooth swing to return the serve deep into your opponent's court, ideally aiming for the back third. This type of return minimizes your opponent's chances of hitting a winning shot off your return. On the other hand, responding to a powerful serve requires quick reflexes and the ability to redirect the energy of the serve. Here, using a firm wrist and a blocked paddle angle can help you deflect the ball back effectively, maintaining both speed and direction and possibly catching your opponent off guard.

Strategic placement of returns is where you can really start to turn the tide. One effective strategy is to aim your returns deep to the baseline. This move forces the server to hit their next shot from a less advantageous position, buying you time to set up for the next play. Alternatively, aiming your returns to the sidelines can stretch your opponent across the court, disrupting their positioning and potentially opening up the court for your next shot. Another great strategy is to hit to the middle of the court. Returning to the middle cuts down the angles on your opponent's third shot, making it harder for them to place a sharp, angled return.

In some cases, especially if you need more time to advance to the kitchen, a higher, slower return can be useful. While it may give your opponent a chance to set up a shot, the extra time it gives you to move forward and establish position at the kitchen can be a worthwhile trade-off, particularly for players with mobility challenges.

The key here is to keep your returns varied and unpredictable, which can frustrate and tire your opponent over the course of the match.

Drills for Returning Serves

Practice drills are invaluable for enhancing your ability to return serves under different scenarios. Set up a drill where a partner serves you a variety of serves—soft, hard, angled, and straight. Your task is to return each serve with the goal of hitting specific targets within your opponent's court. These targets can be deep corners or just beyond the kitchen line. This drill improves your accuracy and helps you adjust your stance and paddle positioning in real time, simulating match conditions.

Another useful drill involves returning serves while continuously moving. Have a partner serve while you jog from one side of the baseline to the other. The constant movement increases your heart rate and simulates the physical stress of a match. Try to return each serve to a different part of the court, enhancing both your physical stamina and your ability to make quick strategic decisions. This type of drill can dramatically improve how you handle pressure during actual gameplay, making you a more resilient and adaptable player.

By focusing on these strategies and incorporating these drills into your practice sessions, you build the skills and confidence to return serves effectively. Remember, every great return you make can set the tone for the rally, shifting the momentum in your favor. Keep practicing, stay focused, and soon, you'll find yourself returning serves with the precision and strategic foresight of an experienced player.

2.3 The Art of the Volley: Timing and Technique

When you step onto the pickleball court, mastering the volley can significantly elevate your game, transforming defensive plays into scoring opportunities. The volley, a stroke performed before the ball bounces, requires not just quick reflexes but a deep understanding of its mechanics. Let's break down these elements to help you refine your volleying skills.

Firstly, the mechanics of a successful volley start with your paddle position and body stance. Your paddle should be held in a **ready position**, ideally waist-high and in front of your body, allowing for rapid, reactive movements. The grip on your paddle during a volley should be firm yet relaxed enough to maneuver quickly, adapting to the speed and angle of the incoming ball. As for your body stance, balance is key. Position your feet shoulder-width apart with a slight bend in the knees, keeping your weight on the balls of your feet. This stance enhances your ability to move laterally or forward with agility, crucial for effective volleying. Timing is another critical component. The ideal moment to strike is when the ball is in front of you, allowing for maximum control over the direction and speed of your return. A well-timed volley is not just about hitting the ball; it's about dictating the pace and direction of the game. Finally, pay close attention to your foot placement near the kitchen, as stepping on or into the kitchen line while making contact with the ball will result in a fault.

Strategically placing your volleys can significantly disrupt your opponent's game plan. One effective strategy is to aim your volleys away from your opponent, making it difficult for them to reach and return the ball. Angling your volleys can also be a game-changer. By directing your volleys at sharp angles, you force your opponent to cover more of the court, which can lead to errors or weaker returns from them. Additionally, varying the depth and speed of your volleys keeps your opponent guessing, preventing them from settling into a predictable rhythm. For instance, a soft volley into the kitchen might bring your opponent closer to the net, setting them up to receive a deeper, more aggressive volley on the next shot. The key is to keep your volleys thoughtful and varied, using each stroke as a strategic tool to control the game.

Timing Drills to Master the Volley

Consider engaging in rapid volley exchanges with a partner to enhance your volleying timing and reflexes. Stand just beyond the kitchen in your volley stance, and have your partner feed you volleys at different speeds and angles. The goal is to return each volley directly to your partner, focusing on maintaining control and accuracy despite the increased pace. This drill not only improves your hand-eye coordination but also your ability to adjust your paddle position quickly and accurately under pressure.

Another valuable drill is reaction training. Have your partner randomly hit balls over the net from close proximity, requiring you to react and volley the ball back swiftly. This drill simulates the unpredictability of game situations, enhancing your reflexes and your ability to perform under pressure. Incorporating these drills into your practice sessions will build the muscle memory and confidence needed to execute precise volleys during critical moments of your matches.

Volleying, like any skill, can sometimes be marred by common errors, particularly when learning or under pressure. One typical mistake is hitting the volley too hard, often sending the ball sailing out of bounds or giving your opponent an easy setup. Focus on controlling the speed of your volley; sometimes, a softer touch is more effective than a hard hit. Another frequent error is failing to step into the volley. While stepping into every shot isn't always necessary or possible, doing so when you can add power and precision to your volleys. Practice stepping towards the ball as you hit your volleys, ensuring your body weight moves from your back foot to your front foot. This forward motion can add force to your shots while maintaining control.

By understanding the mechanics behind effective volleying and practicing strategically, you can turn this swift, reactive stroke into a powerful part of your pickleball repertoire. Remember, the volley isn't just about hitting the ball before it bounces; it's a calculated move that, when executed with precision and thoughtfulness, can significantly influence the game's outcome. Keep practicing, stay mindful of your body mechanics and the strategic placement of your shots, and watch as your volleys transform from defensive returns to proactive game-changers.

2.4 Effective Groundstrokes: Forehand and Backhand

Groundstrokes form the backbone of any pickleball player's game. Whether you are rallying from the baseline or setting up a strategic shot near the net, the quality of your forehand and backhand can often dictate the pace and outcome of the game. Let's explore the fundamental techniques for effective forehand and backhand strokes and how you can develop these to enhance your overall play.

The fundamentals of stroke technique begin with the correct grip. For both the forehand and backhand, a continental grip (where the base knuckle of the index finger is placed on the first bevel of the paddle handle) offers a versatile base from which to execute most shots. This grip aids in stabilizing the paddle during fast exchanges and allows for quick switches between forehand and backhand without significant adjustments. When executing a forehand, your body should be sideways to the net with your feet approximately shoulder-width apart, allowing for optimal balance and power generation. As you prepare to strike the ball, rotate your hips and shoulders back, then uncoil them as you swing, transferring your body weight from your back foot to your front foot. The swing path should be fluid from low to high, with your paddle finishing high and over your shoulder to ensure power and control.

The backhand stroke shares many mechanics with the forehand but requires its own considerations. When preparing for a backhand, the paddle hand should cross your body; the same hip and shoulder rotation is necessary to generate power. However, because the backhand often feels less natural to many players, extra attention should be paid to maintaining a firm wrist and using the body's rotation to generate power rather than relying solely on arm strength.

Improving stroke power and accuracy involves more than arm strength; it encompasses your entire body's mechanics and how effectively you can transfer energy through your paddle. Core strength plays a pivotal role in this energy transfer. Exercises like planks, Russian twists, and medicine ball throws can strengthen your core, providing stability and power during your stroke execution. Proper rotation of the body is equally crucial. Practice rotating your torso during your stroke instead of swinging with just your arms. This full-body movement helps you achieve deeper, more powerful shots while reducing the risk of injury.

Drills for Perfecting Strokes

To refine both your forehand and backhand, regular practice focused on consistency and placement is essential. A simple yet effective drill is the cross-court rally, where you and a partner hit alternating forehand and backhand shots, aiming to keep the ball within specific areas of the court. This drill improves your stroke accuracy and helps develop muscle memory for efficiently switching between forehand and backhand. For a more advanced drill, set up targets in various parts of the court and practice hitting them with both forehand and backhand strokes from different distances. This practice not only sharpens your accuracy but also enhances your ability to adjust your stroke power based on your position relative to the net and your opponent.

Correcting common stroke mistakes is crucial in developing a reliable and effective groundstroke. One of the most common mistakes is over-swinging, where too much force leads to losing control and accuracy. If you frequently miss your target or hit the ball too long, focus on shortening your swing and using more of your body's rotation to generate power. Another frequent error is improper foot alignment, which can throw off your balance and the direction of your stroke. Always ensure your feet are properly positioned before you swing: your toes should be pointing diagonally toward the net on the forehands and more toward the side fence on the backhands. This alignment helps maintain balance and directs your power forward, making your strokes powerful and precise.

Focusing on these foundational techniques and incorporating targeted drills into your practice sessions can significantly enhance the effectiveness of your groundstrokes. As you become more comfortable with the mechanics of each stroke and start correcting common errors, you'll notice a marked improvement in your ability to control rallies and dictate the pace of the game. Remember, consistency is key in pickleball, and a reliable forehand and backhand can be your greatest assets on the court.

2.5 Introduction to Dinking: Why, When, and How

In the dynamic pickleball landscape, mastering the dink shot can significantly elevate your strategic gameplay. Dinking isn't just about gently tapping the ball; it's a nuanced technique designed to extend rallies, create openings, and provoke errors from opponents.

Understanding the why, when, and how of dinking can transform this seemingly simple shot into a powerful part of your game arsenal.

The primary purpose of dinking is to keep the ball low over the net and land it softly in the kitchen. This area is crucial because players cannot volley within this zone, forcing them to let the ball bounce first. By executing a successful dink, you pull your opponent forward into the court, disrupting their position and limiting their ability to hit aggressive, attacking shots. This tactical move can lead to errors from your opponent or create openings for you to exploit with more aggressive shots as the rally progresses. Dinking effectively turns the pace of the game to your advantage, allowing you to control the tempo and draw opponents into playing the game on your terms.

When discussing techniques for an effective dink, several elements come into play. The paddle angle is critical; you want to open the face of your paddle slightly to ensure the ball travels upwards over the net but lands softly in the kitchen. Your grip on the paddle should be gentle yet firm enough to offer control. A death grip on the paddle can send the ball flying, which is counterproductive for dinking. The swing should be controlled and minimal. Think of it more as a push than a hit, using just enough motion to guide the ball over the net and into the desired area. Precision here is key, as the goal is to make the ball barely clear the net but still fall short enough to challenge your opponent effectively.

The situational use of dinks in a game often depends on your opponent's positioning and your strategic objectives. Dinks are most effective when your opponent is positioned at the baseline or mid-court, as it forces them to move forward, potentially pulling them out of their comfort zone. Integrating dinks into your game strategy involves recognizing the right moments to employ them. During a fast-paced volley exchange, for instance, introducing a sudden dink can catch a hard-hitting opponent off guard, shifting the momentum of the game. Additionally, when you notice an opponent struggling with mobility or having difficulty with shots close to the net, regular dinking can be an effective way to exploit these weaknesses.

Dinking Practice Drills

Specific drills can be exceptionally beneficial for honing your dinking skills. One effective drill is the "Dink Rally," where you and a partner exclusively exchange dinks, aiming to keep the ball in the kitchen without it bouncing twice or going out of bounds. This drill helps improve your precision and control, teaching you to manage the pace and placement of the ball effectively. Another useful practice is target dinking. Set small targets within the kitchen, such as bright cones or markers, and practice hitting them with your dinks. This drill not only sharpens your accuracy but also enhances your ability to place the ball strategically during games.

Engaging regularly in these drills can significantly improve your confidence and competence with dinking. As you practice, focus on the smoothness of your paddle movement and the consistency of your ball placement. Over time, these elements will become instinctual, allowing you to integrate dinking into your broader playing strategy seamlessly. Remember, the best dinks are not just about keeping the ball in play; they are about setting yourself up for the next shot, dictating the pace of the rally, and ultimately, controlling the game. By mastering the art of dinking, you equip yourself with a subtle yet powerful tool that enhances your defensive and offensive game, making you a more formidable and strategic player on the court.

2.6 Footwork Fundamentals: Moving Efficiently on the Court

In pickleball, as in life, a solid foundation enables confident movement and effective action. This principle holds especially true when it comes to footwork on the court. Mastering the way you move can elevate your game from good to great, enhancing your ability to reach and return shots, reducing your risk of injury, and improving your overall agility. Think of footwork as the unsung hero of pickleball – it might not get as much attention as a powerful serve or a cunning dink, but it's just as crucial to your success and safety.

The importance of proper footwork cannot be overstated. Efficient movement helps you conserve energy, reach balls more quickly, and position yourself optimally to make effective shots. Furthermore, good footwork decreases your risk of falls and injuries by keeping your body balanced and ready to move in any direction at a moment's notice. It also significantly boosts your reaction time, allowing you to respond swiftly to your opponent's shots and turn potential defensive positions into opportunities for offensive play.

Now, let's break down the basic footwork techniques essential for effectively covering the court. The shuffle step is a fundamental move where you slide your feet sideways without crossing them. This step is crucial for lateral movement across the court, helping you maintain balance and readiness while moving from side to side. Lateral moves involve quick side steps that allow you to cover short distances rapidly, essential during fast-paced volleys. Lastly, quick pivots are necessary for changing directions swiftly; this move involves turning your body quickly to face the new direction while keeping one foot in place as a pivot point.

Footwork Drills to Enhance Agility

Incorporating specific drills into your practice sessions can be incredibly beneficial for improving your agility and footwork. One effective drill is the ladder drill, where a sports ladder (see image) is laid flat on the court to practice different footwork patterns. For example, you can practice the "in-and-out" drill, where you step into each box of the ladder with both feet and then step out sideways, alternating the lead foot each time. This drill enhances your ability to move quickly and accurately, crucial for responding to game situations.

Another valuable exercise is the cone drill, which involves setting up cones in various patterns on the court. For example, you might set them up in a zigzag pattern and practice running quickly between them while maintaining control and balance. This drill not only improves your speed and agility but also your ability to change direction quickly—an invaluable skill during intense pickleball rallies.

Common Footwork Mistakes and Corrections

Even seasoned players can find themselves making footwork errors, which can hinder their gameplay. A common mistake is overstepping, where players take larger steps than necessary. This can lead to loss of balance and slower movement. To correct this, practice taking smaller, more controlled steps during drills. Focus on keeping your steps quick and light, which will help you maintain balance and readiness to change direction quickly.

Another frequent issue is poor balance, often caused by inadequate foot positioning. Poor balance can make it difficult to execute shots effectively and lead to falls. To improve balance, work on drills that require you to move quickly while maintaining control, such as the cone drill mentioned earlier. Additionally, consider incorporating balance-specific exercises into your training regimen, such as standing on one leg or using a balance board.

You'll move more confidently and efficiently on the court by dedicating time to practicing these footwork fundamentals and correcting common errors. Effective footwork is key to reaching your full potential in pickleball, enabling you to handle fast-paced exchanges, navigate the court effortlessly, and react swiftly to your opponent's moves. As you refine your footwork, you'll see improvements in your gameplay and enjoy a greater sense of control and confidence during matches.

Skinny Singles: A Footwork Drill for Precision and Control

Skinny singles in pickleball is a practice drill where two players compete in a singles format, but each player is restricted to using only one side of the court. Here's how it works:

- **Court Setup**: Instead of using the full singles court, each player is restricted to one side of the court (either the right or left half). Both players can agree to play on the diagonal halves or the straight vertical halves.

- **Rules**: Players can only hit shots into the designated half of the court, and all the normal pickleball rules apply. The drill can be played using regular singles or doubles scoring.

Skinny singles is a highly effective drill for improving precision, movement, and control by requiring players to hit into a smaller target area. It also enhances positioning and strategy, making it beneficial for both singles and doubles play.

As we wrap up this chapter on developing your skills, remember that each technique, from serving to footwork, builds upon the others to enhance your overall game. The skills you've learned here form the foundation for building more advanced strategies and playstyles. In the next chapter, we'll delve into strategic play, helping you integrate these skills into a cohesive game plan that maximizes your strengths and challenges your opponents. Keep practicing, stay focused, and prepare to take your game to the next level.

Chapter Three

Advanced Techniques and Strategies

As you continue exploring the world of pickleball, mastering the basics sets you up perfectly to explore more complex and nuanced aspects of the game. Advanced techniques enhance your skill set and enrich your playing experience, allowing you to engage in the game with a new level of finesse and strategy. This chapter is dedicated to elevating your game through advanced techniques and strategies, starting with the serve—a fundamental stroke that sets the tone for every point and significantly influences the outcome of the game. Consider your serve as your first line of offense and a crucial strategic move in the complex dance of a pickleball rally. Mastering these advanced elements will enhance your overall performance and navigate each rally with greater skill and insight.

3.1 Advanced Serving Techniques: Adding Spin and Power

Incorporating Spin into Serves

One of the most effective ways to elevate your serving game is to introduce **spin**. Spin affects the ball's trajectory and bounce, adding a layer of complexity that can confuse and complicate the receiver's return. **Topspin** and **backspin** are two fundamental types of spin you can apply to your serves. When you impart topspin on the ball, you strike it so it rotates forward rapidly. This rotation causes the ball to dip down faster than it normally would, making it difficult for the receiver to judge where it will land and how it will bounce. Conversely, backspin, or underspin, involves striking the ball so that it spins backward. This type of spin causes the ball to bounce lower and slower, potentially throwing off your opponent's timing and response.

To effectively apply spin to your serves, focus on the point of contact. For topspin, angle your paddle slightly upward and strike the ball in an upward motion, grazing the bottom half of the ball to generate forward rotation. For backspin on a drop serve, angle your paddle slightly downward and strike the top half of the ball in a downward motion. The key to successful spin is wrist movement—snap your wrist as you hit the ball to maximize the spin. With practice, these serves can become powerful tools in your serving arsenal, giving you an edge right from the start of the rally.

Power Serve Techniques

While spin serves rely on finesse, power serves depend on strength and speed. A well-executed power serve can overwhelm your opponent, earning you easy points or forcing weak returns that set you up for a winning follow-up shot. The mechanics behind a powerful serve involve optimal body alignment, paddle speed, and the point of contact. Stand with your feet shoulder-width apart, parallel to the baseline. As you prepare to serve, rotate your hips and shoulders back, then swiftly rotate them forward as you swing, channeling the power from your core through your arm and into the paddle. Strike the ball at the highest comfortable point in front of you to maximize the power and downward angle of your serve, ensuring it clears the net but stays within the bounds of the service box.

Serving Placement Strategy

Strategic placement of your serves can significantly disrupt your opponent's game plan. You can gain the upper hand by targeting weak spots in their positioning or playing style. For instance, if your opponent struggles with backhand returns, consistently serving deep to their backhand can force errors or weak returns. Alternatively, mixing up your serve placement—serving deep one time, then short the next—can prevent your opponent guessing and prevent them from getting into a comfortable rhythm.

Drills for Perfecting Advanced Serves

To master these advanced serving techniques, specific drills can be incredibly beneficial. Set up targets in different areas of the service box to practice your accuracy with both spin and power serves. Use markers to designate target zones for deep and short serves, and practice hitting these targets with varying spins and speeds. Additionally, you can practice serving under different conditions to simulate match scenarios. For instance, practice your serves when you're slightly fatigued or under mild stress to mimic the physical and mental conditions of a competitive match. This type of practice improves your technical skills and enhances your ability to execute these serves reliably under pressure.

By integrating these advanced serving techniques into your practice routines, you're not just working on hitting the ball over the net—you're learning to start each point with a purpose. Whether it's gaining an immediate advantage with a powerful strike or setting up a strategic rally with a well-placed spin serve, these advanced techniques can transform your serve into a dynamic and formidable weapon in your pickleball arsenal. As you continue to refine these skills, remember that consistency is key. The more you practice, the more natural these advanced serves will feel during games, allowing you to serve with confidence and strategic intent.

3.2 Defensive Plays: Techniques to Turn the Game

In pickleball, a well-rounded player knows that defense is just as crucial as offense. It's not just about how aggressively you can play; your ability to defend effectively can often be the difference between winning and losing a point. A robust defensive strategy relies heavily on anticipation and reaction skills. Anticipation in pickleball involves reading your opponent's body language and paddle position, allowing you to predict where the next shot will land. This skill does not develop overnight but grows as you gain more experience and insight into the game's strategic nuances. For instance, a player who consistently looks at their target before hitting usually plans a straightforward shot, whereas a sudden lack of eye contact might precede a deceptive shot. By observing these subtle cues, you can position yourself optimally and prepare your response, turning what could be a defensive scramble into a controlled counterattack.

Moreover, enhancing your reaction skills is crucial for effective defense. These skills hinge not only on physical speed but also on your ability to remain calm and focused under pressure. The key is maintaining a balanced stance with your knees slightly bent and your paddle ready at chest height, allowing quick movements in any direction. This readiness, combined with acute mental alertness, enables you to respond swiftly to unexpected shots, turning potential points for your opponent into opportunities for you to regain control of the play.

Effective Use of Lobs and Resets

Two of the most strategic defensive shots in pickleball are the lob and the **reset shot**. The defensive lob is particularly useful when you are out of position or under pressure. Lobbing the ball high and deep into your opponent's court gives you time to recover and return to a favorable position. The key to a successful defensive lob lies in its placement; aim for the back third of the court to maximize the distance your opponent must cover to return the shot. This placement not only buys you time but also forces your opponent to hit a more challenging overhead return, which could lead to a weaker shot you can exploit.

Reset shots, however, are all about regaining control of the rally. Typically used when the pace of the game becomes too fast and aggressive for your liking, a reset shot is a soft, controlled return that lands in the kitchen, forcing the rally to slow down. The effectiveness of a reset shot lies in its ability to neutralize your opponent's offensive advantage, turning a fast-paced, aggressive rally into a more manageable, slower-paced exchange. To execute a reset shot effectively, use a gentle paddle stroke to cushion the ball, reducing its speed as it crosses the net. Aim for the center of the kitchen to limit your opponent's angle options.

Blocking and Counterattacking

Blocking powerful volleys or drives from your opponent is another critical defensive skill. When you face a fast, aggressive shot, a well-timed **block** can diffuse the attack and keep you in the game. To block effectively, hold your paddle firm and angle it slightly towards the ground, using the ball's momentum to direct it back over the net. This technique stops the ball and sends it back low, making it difficult for your opponent to launch another aggressive shot. The keys to effectively blocking are keeping your body balanced, having a light grip on the paddle, keeping a stable wrist, absorbing the speed of the ball, and keeping your eye on the ball. A good block can be critical in defending against a hard hitter or beating a banger.

Transitioning from blocking to **counterattacking** is where you can truly turn the tide of the game. After a successful block, observe your opponent's position and readiness. It's the perfect time to switch from defense to offense if they are off-balance or out of position. Use a quick, sharp shot aimed away from your opponent to capitalize on their vulnerability, aiming for areas of the court that are difficult for them to cover quickly.

Practice Scenarios for Defensive Mastery

To master these defensive techniques, you must practice them in realistic, high-pressure situations. One effective drill is the "defense to offense" drill. Have a partner or coach deliver a series of aggressive shots towards you, mixing volleys, drives, and smashes. Your goal is to block these shots and immediately counterattack, aiming for precision and placement rather than power. This drill helps you practice your blocking and counterattacking skills and enhances your ability to transition smoothly between defensive and offensive plays.

Another useful drill focuses on lob and reset shot mastery. Begin by engaging in a fast-paced volley exchange with a partner. Randomly, one player switches the rally's pace by introducing a lob or a reset shot. This sudden change requires both players to adjust their strategies quickly, mimicking the unpredictability of match play. This type of practice hones your individual shot techniques and improves your overall adaptability on the court.

Incorporating these advanced defensive strategies and drills into your practice sessions will help you develop a more resilient and versatile game. Defensive skills are not just about stopping your opponent's shots; they're about turning defense into opportunity, allowing you to control the pace and flow of the game, no matter how intense the pressure. With dedication and practice, your defense can become one of the most potent parts of your pickleball gameplay, keeping your opponents guessing and giving you the upper hand in crucial moments.

3.3 Offensive Strategies: Positioning and Attack

When you're ready to take the offensive in pickleball, positioning yourself effectively on the court can dramatically increase your ability to dominate the play. One strategic move is to position yourself aggressively by moving up to the kitchen. This area of the court is a hotbed for quick, sharp exchanges and is crucial for setting up offensive plays. However, timing your advance is key. Typically, you'll move up right after a successful **third shot drop** that lands softly in the opponent's kitchen, compelling them to hit a weak return. As you move up, keep your paddle up and your eyes on the ball, ready to volley with precision. This aggressive positioning puts pressure on your opponents, limiting their shot options and giving you the upper hand in dictating the rally's pace and direction.

Creating openings in your opponent's defense is another critical aspect of offensive play. This strategy involves not only skill and precision but also a bit of cunning. **Feints**, or deceptive moves, can be particularly effective in this regard. A feint might involve pretending to hit a powerful shot and then playing a soft dink instead, causing your opponent to react to the shot you feigned rather than the one you actually made. Quick changes in attack direction also keep your opponent guessing and off-balance. For instance, if you've been hitting several shots to your opponent's forehand, suddenly switching to an unexpected backhand shot can exploit their momentary unpreparedness, creating a valuable opening for you to score.

Combining different shots effectively builds pressure on your opponent and can significantly shift the game's momentum in your favor. A classic combination that works well is the drop shot followed by a drive. Here's how it unfolds: start with a drop shot that gently lands in the kitchen, forcing your opponent to move forward and hit upwards. As they reposition themselves after the drop, you unleash a powerful drive shot aimed deep into the court. This sudden shift from a soft play to an aggressive strike can catch your opponent off-guard, making it difficult for them to defend effectively. This strategy tests your opponent's physical and mental agility as they try to anticipate and react to your varied play.

Ernes and ATPs

Ernes and **Around-The-Post** Shots (ATPs) represent advanced techniques that can elevate your pickleball game to a new level of strategic sophistication. The Erne, named after its creator, is a daring and strategic maneuver where a player jumps over the non-volley zone (also known as the kitchen) or moves swiftly outside the sideline to hit a ball before it bounces. The key to executing an Erne is positioning yourself out of bounds, re-establishing your feet outside the court, and striking the ball just after it crosses the net. This shot is particularly effective when your opponent least expects it, catching them off guard and potentially earning you a point outright or placing you in a favorable position for the next shot.

ATPs, on the other hand, involve hitting the ball around the net post from a wide angle. This shot requires precise timing and angle calculation, often used when you're forced wide on the court. By utilizing ATPs, you can surprise your opponent with an unexpected angle that bypasses their defensive position, leaving them unable to reach the ball.

Mastering Ernes and ATPs not only adds variety to your offensive arsenal but also disrupts your opponent's rhythm, forcing them to continuously adjust their positioning and defensive strategy. Incorporating these advanced techniques into your game demands practice, anticipation, and the confidence to execute them decisively during critical points in a match. By integrating Ernes and ATPs into your repertoire, you gain the ability to dictate play more effectively, turning defensive situations into offensive opportunities and keeping your opponents guessing throughout the match.

Offensive Drills for Advanced Players

Specific drills can be set up to refine these offensive strategies, mimicking game-like conditions and pressure. For aggressive court positioning, practice the "advance and volley" drill. Start from the baseline, hit a deep shot, and quickly move up to the kitchen line to prepare for a volley. Your partner should return your shot with various angles and speeds, challenging your ability to maintain an aggressive stance and effectively volley from near the net. This drill enhances your ability to control the net area and apply pressure from close range.

Another useful drill focuses on creating and exploiting openings. This can be practiced through the "feint and switch" drill, where you play a series of shots with a partner and intentionally include feints and sudden changes in the direction of your attacks. Begin by establishing a pattern, such as several shots to one side, and then unexpectedly change the pattern with a shot to the opposite side or a sudden drop shot. This drill improves your ability to execute feints convincingly and helps you react to your own changes in strategy, enhancing your adaptability and quick decision-making skills.

For combination shots, the "drop-drive sequence" drill is highly effective. With a partner, continuously alternate between drop shots and drive shots. The goal is to perfect the timing and execution of transitioning from a soft touch to a powerful strike, ensuring each shot sets up the next. This drill not only improves your technical skills in executing both shots but also enhances your strategic understanding of how different shots can be combined for maximum effect on the court.

By integrating these advanced offensive strategies and drills into your practice, you're equipping yourself with the tools needed to control the game and keep your opponents under pressure. Offensive play in pickleball is about much more than just hitting the ball; it's about making strategic decisions that maximize your strengths and exploit your opponent's weaknesses. With consistent practice and strategic play, you can transform your approach from reactive to proactive, dictating the pace and direction of the game to emerge as a dominant force on the court.

3.4 Mastering the Third Shot Drop

The third shot drop in pickleball is arguably one of the pivotal skills that can significantly transform your game, especially in doubles play. It acts as a bridge, allowing you to transition from the baseline to the net—a territory where many points are won. This shot is crucial because it's typically used to counter your opponent's deep return of your serve. Instead of returning with a powerful drive that they can easily volley back, the third shot drop offers a softer, more strategic alternative. By dropping the ball just over the net into the kitchen, you force your opponent to move forward, hit upward, and ideally set up a more advantageous scenario for your next move.

Executing an effective third shot drop involves a blend of precision, timing, and understanding of paddle angles. The goal is to strike the ball softly enough to arc over the net and land in the non-volley zone, making it difficult for your opponents to return with power. To achieve this, your paddle angle is critical. You'll want to open the face of your paddle slightly, aiming to hit the ball with a gentle upward trajectory. Positioning is also crucial; stand about midway between the baseline and the net to give yourself enough distance to loft the ball gently into the kitchen. The timing of your swing should synchronize closely with the peak of the ball's bounce – hitting it too early or too late could send it sailing into the net or too far into your opponent's court.

The effectiveness of the third shot drop doesn't just hinge on your ability to perform the shot technically but also on reading the game and understanding when and where to use it. For instance, if your opponents are hanging back near the baseline, a well-placed third shot drop can draw them out of position, disrupting their defensive setup and making them vulnerable to subsequent attacks. Conversely, if they are already positioned near the net, a third shot drop can force them to retreat or create uncertainty, disrupting their rhythm and control of the net.

Practice Drills for the Third Shot Drop

To truly integrate the third shot drop into your repertoire, targeted practice is essential. One effective drill is the "kitchen drop drill," where you and a partner rally focus solely on dropping shots into each other's kitchens. Start from the baseline and work on dropping the ball into the kitchen with varying degrees of spin and speed. This helps improve your accuracy and ability to judge the force behind each shot, depending on your position on the court.

Another dynamic drill to enhance your third shot drop skills involves practicing under simulated match pressures. Have a partner or coach feed you shots at varying depths and speeds, mimicking a real game scenario. Your task is to respond with third shot drops, aiming to land them just over the net in the kitchen. To add complexity, your partner can vary their responses, sometimes rushing to the net and other times staying back, forcing you to quickly assess the best strategic use of the third shot drop based on their position.

Integrating these drills into your regular practice sessions will boost your confidence in executing the third shot drop and enhance your strategic understanding of when and how to use this shot effectively. As you continue to refine this skill, you'll find yourself better equipped to control the pace and flow of the game, making strategic advances to the net more fluid and securing points more efficiently. The third shot drop, while seemingly simple, is a testament to the nuanced strategy at the heart of pickleball, encapsulating the blend of finesse, timing, and tactical acumen that the sport demands.

3.5 Winning with the Kitchen: Strategies for the Non-Volley Zone

The kitchen is a pivotal area in pickleball, where games can be won or lost. Dominating this zone is about more than just avoiding volleys; it's about mastering a range of techniques that allow you to control the pace and flow of the game. Effective kitchen play involves utilizing quick returns, precise dinks, and strategic blocks to maintain pressure on your opponent and limit their offensive options.

Quick volleys near the kitchen require fast reflexes and the ability to predict your opponent's next move. When you're positioned near the kitchen line, keep your paddle up, and your eyes focused on the ball, ready to intercept it quickly and volley it back into your opponent's kitchen area. This kind of rapid exchange can be intense. Still, by keeping the ball low and aiming just over the net, you increase the difficulty of your opponent's return, potentially leading to their making a mistake or giving you a more attackable ball on their return.

Dinking is another critical skill for kitchen dominance. The soft, controlled touch of a dink forces your opponent to move forward and hit upward, limiting their ability to generate powerful returns. When dinking, aim for the corners of the kitchen to maximize the distance your opponent must cover, thereby increasing the chance of a mistake on their part. The subtlety of a well-placed dink can disrupt even the most aggressive opponent's rhythm, turning the tide of the game in your favor.

Strategic blocks are also essential when playing in the kitchen. If your opponent manages to escalate the pace, a well-timed block can slow down the rally and give you control of the play. Use a firm wrist and a stable paddle to block the ball softly back into the kitchen, aiming for areas that are difficult for your opponent to reach. This keeps you in the play and can set you up for a more aggressive follow-up shot.

Transitioning effectively into and out of the kitchen is as crucial as the shots you play within it. This movement must be fluid and strategic, allowing you to approach the net for a volley or dink and then move back to a more defensive position as needed. The key to effective transitioning is to move in sync with the rhythm of the game—advance as you see an opportunity to apply pressure or execute a winning shot, and retreat when it's necessary to defend against your opponent's attacks. Always keep your paddle ready and your feet moving, and use lateral steps to maintain your balance and readiness.

Kitchen Line Strategies

Mastering the edges of the non-volley zone can give you a distinct advantage. One effective tactic is to play close to the kitchen line, which allows you to volley legally while keeping the pressure on your opponent. When playing these shots, ensure that your feet do not touch the line or enter the kitchen before or during contact with the ball. Additionally, be mindful that your momentum cannot carry you into the kitchen even after completing the shot, as this would result in a fault. This positioning allows you to reach balls that are dropping close to the net and to angle your volleys sharply across the court.

Another strategy is to exploit the boundaries of the kitchen by using wide angles and sharp **crosscourt** dinks. These shots force your opponents to cover more ground and can lead to them making hurried, imprecise returns. By consistently pushing the limits of the space your opponent must defend, you can create openings for more definitive shots that can end the rally in your favor.

Drills for Mastering Kitchen Play

To hone your kitchen skills, consider drills that focus on speed, accuracy, and strategic shot selection. One effective drill is the "kitchen exchange," where players rally exclusively within the kitchen, focusing on dinks, volleys, and blocks. The goal is to maintain control of the rally by keeping the ball low and placing it strategically within the opponent's kitchen area. Another useful drill is the 'line dance,' where you practice your footwork along the kitchen line, volleying and dinking without stepping into the kitchen. This drill improves your balance and precision, teaching you to manage the spatial constraints of the non-volley zone while executing effective shots.

By mastering these strategies and incorporating rigorous practice drills, you enhance your ability to control the kitchen and, by extension, the game. The non-volley zone may seem like just a small part of the court, but its strategic importance is immense. Whether you're volleying, dinking, or blocking, remember that each shot played near the kitchen can significantly impact the rally's outcome. You can turn the kitchen into your stronghold with practice and strategic awareness, commanding the game and leading yourself to victory.

3.6 Singles vs. Doubles: Tailored Strategies for Each Game Type

When it comes to pickleball, the strategic nuances of singles and doubles play are as distinct as they are fascinating. Each format requires a unique set of strategies and a tailored approach to the game that leverages personal strengths and team dynamics. Let's dive into the strategies that can elevate your game in both singles and doubles play, ensuring you're as effective on the court as possible, regardless of the format.

Strategies Unique to Singles Play

In singles, the game becomes a test of endurance, skill, and strategic acumen, with each player covering the entire court on their own. Stamina management becomes crucial in singles play. Unlike doubles, where responsibilities can be shared, singles require you to be in constant motion, often sprinting from one end of the court to the other. Effective stamina management involves physical fitness and the strategic conservation of energy during play. This might mean choosing moments when it's advantageous to unleash high-energy bursts and times when a more measured approach is prudent.

The use of the whole court in singles is also strategic. With no partner to cover half the court, you need to make every inch of your side work for you. This involves playing shots that move your opponent around the court as much as possible, exploiting gaps, and using deep shots to push them back, paired with short shots to draw them forward. Aggressive shot-making is another key strategy in singles. Without the risk of hitting a partner, you can often afford to make bolder plays. Sharp angles, powerful drives, and strategic placements can all be used more freely, allowing you to challenge your opponent on every point.

Doubles Coordination and Communication

Switching to doubles play, the game shifts dramatically. Coordination and communication become the linchpins of a successful doubles team. Positioning in doubles is less about covering the whole court individually and more about seamless teamwork. This involves understanding shared responsibilities and moving in a synchronized manner. For instance, when one player moves to the net, the other should move in parallel, ensuring that the court is covered efficiently without gaps.

Communication in doubles extends beyond verbal calls. While calling shots and signals are crucial, non-verbal cues like body language and eye contact play significant roles. Establishing clear signals for who will take the shot in different scenarios can prevent collisions and missed opportunities. For example, some teams use paddle signals or specific calls to indicate who will take the serve or return, ensuring clarity even amidst the fast-paced action of a game.

Adapting Play Style Between Singles and Doubles

The transition between singles and doubles play involves physical adjustments and a change in mindset. In singles, the strategy often revolves around personal strength and endurance, while doubles is more about synergy and joint tactics. Adapting from an individualistic approach in singles to a team-focused strategy in doubles is crucial. For instance, aggressive net play might work well in singles but could expose gaps in a doubles formation if not executed in concert with your partner.

In doubles, you also need to adapt your shot selection to accommodate and complement your partner's style and position. This might mean setting up shots your partner can capitalize on rather than going for outright **winners**, as you might in singles. Conversely, when moving from doubles to singles, the focus shifts back to maximizing personal skill and court coverage, requiring a more self-reliant and exhaustive approach to each point.

Tailored Drills for Singles and Doubles

To effectively enhance skills relevant to both singles and doubles, tailored drills can play a pivotal role. For singles, drills that emphasize stamina and court coverage are beneficial.

One effective drill is the "baseline to net sprint", where you hit a shot from the baseline and then sprint to the net to make a volley, mimicking the rapid change of position often required in singles play.

For doubles, drills that focus on coordination and situational play are ideal. "Role reversal" drills, where players switch their usual positions, can be particularly effective in enhancing understanding and adaptability within the team. This helps both players become more versatile and aware of the challenges each position faces, fostering greater empathy and teamwork.

By integrating these tailored strategies and drills into your practice, you can effectively enhance your abilities in both singles and doubles pickleball. Each form of the game offers unique challenges and rewards, pushing you to adapt and grow as a player. Whether you're mastering the art of endurance in singles or the symphony of teamwork in doubles, the skills you develop will not only improve your game but also enrich your enjoyment of this dynamic sport.

With these strategies in your toolkit, you're now better equipped to face any opponent across the net in either singles or doubles play. As we transition into the next chapter, we'll explore how to fine-tune these skills further and apply them in competitive settings, ensuring you're ready to take your game to the next level. Additionally, refer to Appendix B for a more structured practice routine, where you'll find six 30-minute drill sets designed to help you systematically develop and enhance your pickleball skills.

Your Review Matters: Help Spread the Joy of Pickleball

"True happiness comes from helping others." – Dalai Lama

Thank you for joining me on this pickleball adventure! I hope you're enjoying this book as much as I enjoyed writing it. Now, I have a small favor to ask.

Imagine helping another pickleball enthusiast who's eager to start their journey, just like you were. They're looking to learn, improve, and have fun on the court, and your review could be the guiding hand they need.

Here's how you can make a big difference:

Please take a moment to leave a review for this book. It's quick, it's free, and it can help someone else discover the joy of pickleball. Your review could inspire:

- One more person to pick up a paddle and join the game.
- One more beginner to grasp the basics with confidence.
- One more player to improve their skills and enjoy the sport even more.
- One more family to find a new way to bond and stay active.
- One more dream of playing like a pro to become a reality.

Ready to share your thoughts?

Simply click or scan the QR code below to leave your review on Amazon. It only takes a minute, but your impact could last a lifetime.

Chapter Four
Physical Fitness and Nutrition

IMAGINE THIS: YOU'RE IN the middle of a riveting game of pickleball, the score is tight, and every point counts. Suddenly, you realize you're not just battling your opponent but also your own body. You're breathing heavily, your muscles scream with each sprint, and despite the burning desire to clinch the game, your body seems to lag. Now, picture a different scene. You're the same enthusiastic player, but this time, you're breezing across the court with energy to spare, your movements are sharp, and every shot is as vigorous as the first. What makes the difference in these scenarios? It's not just skill or willpower—it's your physical fitness and how you fuel your body. This chapter explores how integrating fitness and proper nutrition can enhance your performance and transform your experience of the game.

4.1 Pickleball as Cardio: How to Maximize Your Workout

Pickleball is more than just a fun activity; it's a dynamic way to improve cardiovascular health. Every sprint, lateral move, and vigorous volley contributes to an elevated heart rate, pushing your cardio endurance and helping you burn calories efficiently. The beauty of pickleball lies in its ability to combine short bursts of high-intensity activity with brief moments of rest, mirroring the principles of interval training. This natural stop-and-start pattern is not just a gameplay feature; it enhances heart health and boosts metabolic rates more effectively than steady-state cardio exercises.

The key to maximizing these cardiovascular benefits lies in engaging in the game. For instance, the intensity of your play plays a crucial role. Engaging in more aggressive, fast-paced games increases your heart rate and calorie burn. However, it's crucial to maintain a balance. Monitoring your exertion levels is essential to ensure you're challenging yourself without overdoing it. A practical way to monitor your intensity is to use the 'talk test'; you should be able to speak short sentences while playing, but if you're too breathless to converse, you might be pushing too hard.

To further enhance the cardio benefits, consider your movement on the court. Positioning yourself strategically and choosing your shots to maximize court coverage can turn every game into a high-intensity workout. For example, instead of sticking close to the baseline, move up to the non-volley zone to engage in volleys and dinks, which usually require quick, short bursts of energy. This not only makes the game more physically demanding but also develops your agility and reflexes.

Monitoring Intensity

Keeping track of your physical exertion during play can help you maintain the optimal intensity for cardiovascular benefits without risking exhaustion. One effective method is wearing a heart rate monitor during games. This device can provide real-time feedback on your heart rate zones, helping you stay within a target range that maximizes cardiorespiratory benefits while keeping the activity safe and enjoyable. Aim to keep your heart rate within 50-70% of your maximum during moderate play and 70-85% during more vigorous sessions. These ranges help improve your heart health and endurance, ensuring you perform better and enjoy each game to the fullest.

Engaging in pickleball as a form of cardio exercise offers a fun and social way to enhance your fitness. It allows you to enjoy the competitive spirit of the game while reaping significant health benefits. You can transform your pickleball sessions into effective cardiovascular workouts by understanding and implementing strategies to maximize movement and monitor intensity. This approach improves your game and contributes significantly to your overall health, ensuring that each match enhances your physical well-being, keeping you swift, sharp, and competitive on the court.

4.2 Strength Training for Pickleball Players

Building strength is not just about enhancing your power; it's about creating a resilient body that can endure the rigors of pickleball while minimizing the risk of injury. When you strengthen the muscles used most frequently in pickleball—namely your core, legs, and arms—you improve your game performance and protect your body from the strains and stresses of repetitive motion. Let's discuss how you can develop these crucial muscle groups through targeted exercises, seamlessly integrate strength training into your routine, and balance it with flexibility exercises for optimal athletic performance.

The core muscles, which include your abdominals, lower back, and obliques, are central to almost every movement in pickleball. A strong core stabilizes your body, allowing for more powerful and controlled movements while reducing the torque placed on your spine. Exercises like planks, Russian twists, and medicine ball slams can significantly enhance your core strength. For instance, holding a plank for increasing periods helps build endurance in your core muscles, while Russian twists, involving a twisting motion with a medicine ball, engage and strengthen your obliques, crucial for those quick, twisting shots during a game.

Planks and Russian Twists

Your legs also play a pivotal role in pickleball, providing the power behind your sprints and lunges and the stability needed for quick changes in direction. Focus on exercises like squats, lunges, and calf raises to build leg strength. Squats strengthen your glutes, hamstrings, and quadriceps, all vital for explosive movements. Lunges are particularly beneficial for improving balance, flexibility, and strength, mimicking the forward movement often required in pickleball. Calf raises, on the other hand, enhance the ability of your lower legs to propel you into a sprint or support you as you reach for a low shot.

Squats, Lunges, and Calf Raises

Arm strength is crucial for powerful serves and returns. However, it's important to focus on both power and endurance. Incorporating exercises like bicep curls, tricep dips, and shoulder presses will help you build the arm strength you need for those powerful shots. Moreover, resistance bands can add variety to your workout, helping to improve both strength and flexibility. Bands can be used for a range of exercises that mimic the movements of pickleball, providing resistance that helps strengthen the muscle groups most engaged during play.

Bicep Curls, Triceps Dips, and Shoulder Presses

Integrating strength training into your regular fitness routine doesn't mean you must spend hours in the gym. In fact, short, focused sessions several times a week can be more effective. Aim for at least two strength training sessions per week, focusing on the key muscle groups involved in pickleball. Each session doesn't need to be lengthy; even 20-30 minutes can be sufficient if your exercises are targeted and performed with enough intensity. For detailed exercise instructions, please refer to Appendix C. It's also crucial to schedule these sessions on days when you're not playing pickleball, allowing your body time to recover and prevent overuse injuries.

The balance between strength and flexibility is vital for any athlete, but it's particularly crucial in a sport like pickleball, where quick, multidirectional movements are common. Strength training can sometimes lead to shortened, tight muscles, so it's important to complement your strength workouts with flexibility exercises. This balance helps prevent injuries and ensures your movements on the court are fluid and efficient. Incorporate dynamic stretches before your strength training to warm up your muscles and static stretches after your workout to enhance flexibility and aid recovery. These practices ensure that your muscles remain strong, supple, and responsive to the demands of pickleball.

By focusing on these aspects of strength training, you're not just preparing your body for the specific demands of pickleball but also enhancing your overall health and athletic performance. The key is consistency and balance—regularly engaging in these exercises while ensuring you're not overloading your body on any given day. With a well-rounded approach to strength and flexibility, you'll find yourself moving more confidently on the court, powered by a strong and agile body, ready to meet any challenge your opponent might throw your way.

4.3 Flexibility and Mobility Exercises to Enhance Game Performance

Enhancing your flexibility and mobility can significantly elevate your pickleball game by enabling smoother movements, a broader range of motion, and a drastic reduction in the risk of injuries. When you can move with greater ease and less discomfort, your performance on the court improves, and your recovery time shortens, allowing you to play more frequently and with consistent intensity.

For most pickleball players, the key areas to focus on are the hips, shoulders, and back, each of which is heavily engaged during intense play.

<u>Hips</u>: Start with the hips, which are crucial for nearly all pickleball movements, from lateral runs to forward lunges. Tight hips can severely limit your range of motion, impacting your ability to reach low shots or quickly change directions. Exercises like hip circles and pigeon poses can greatly enhance hip flexibility, making your movements more fluid and less prone to strains.

Hip Circles and Pigeon Poses

Shoulders: The shoulders endure continuous racket swinging, so incorporating stretches such as arm circles and the cross-body shoulder stretch can help maintain mobility and reduce stiffness. This ensures your swings remain powerful and pain-free.

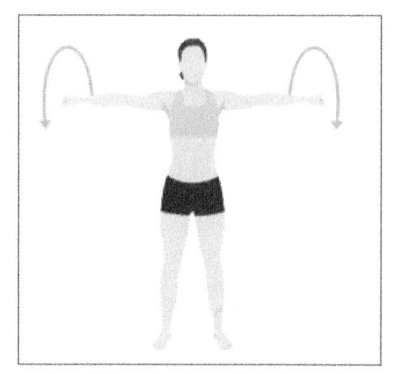

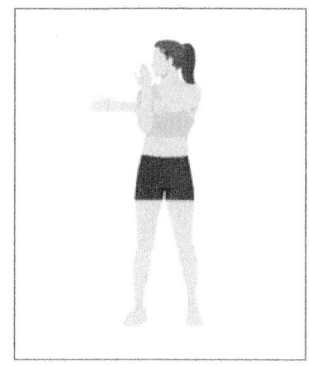

Arm Circles and Cross Body Stretches

Back: The back, especially the lower back, plays a pivotal role in maintaining posture and balance during the game. Activities like the cat-cow stretch or gentle spinal twists can help keep your back supple and resilient, warding off the typical soreness that comes from hours of play. Regularly implementing these targeted stretches enhances flexibility and bolsters core stability, crucial for powerful and controlled movements on the court.

Cat Cow and Spinal Twists

Dynamic vs. Static Stretching

Understanding when to use dynamic versus static stretching can optimize your performance and prevent injuries. Dynamic stretches involve controlled movements that prepare your muscles, ligaments, and other soft tissues for optimal performance and injury prevention. They are ideal before you start playing, as they warm up the muscles, making them more elastic and ready for the demands of pickleball. Examples include leg swings, which prepare your hips and legs for the dynamic movements of a game, and arm swings, which loosen up the shoulders and upper back.

On the other hand, static stretching is usually performed at the end of your play session. This type of stretching involves holding a stretch for a period of time, which helps to lengthen muscles and improve flexibility. It also promotes relaxation and reduces the risk of injury. Static stretching aids in cooling down your body, relaxing your muscles, and increasing your flexibility over time.

Implementing both types of stretching in your routine ensures that your muscles are prepped before playing and properly cooled down afterward, reducing your risk of injuries like muscle pulls or joint stress. For instance, starting your day with dynamic stretches can invigorate your body and boost your flexibility, providing an excellent kickoff to a pickleball session. Following up with static stretches post-game can aid muscle recovery and prevent stiffness, keeping you in top form.

Routine Development

Developing a consistent flexibility routine is essential for maintaining the range of motion necessary for effective pickleball play. Such a routine should ideally be tailored to fit your playing schedule, physical needs, and fitness goals. For players who engage in pickleball multiple times a week, integrating a 10-15 minute flexibility session into your daily routine can work wonders. This session could include a combination of dynamic stretches as part of your warm-up before games and static stretches to cool down. For a detailed 10-15 minute flexibility session, please refer to Appendix D.

To make this routine more effective, focus on stretches that target the muscle groups most used in pickleball, ensuring they remain agile and ready for the sport's quick, multidirectional movements. Additionally, incorporating yoga or Pilates sessions into your weekly schedule can further enhance your flexibility, providing a comprehensive workout that benefits both mind and body.

By prioritizing flexibility and mobility through dedicated exercises and a well-structured routine, you enhance your ability to perform and protect your body from the wear and tear of regular play. This proactive approach to fitness ensures that each game of pickleball is as enjoyable as it is competitive, keeping you agile, alert, and ready to dominate the court.

4.4 Injury Prevention: Tips and Exercises

While less intense than some racket sports, pickleball still poses its own set of physical demands and risks. Common injuries such as ankle sprains, shoulder strains, and even wrist injuries can occur, often due to quick changes in direction, repetitive arm movements, and the impact of hitting the ball. Ankle sprains might result from an awkward landing or a misstep when moving laterally, while shoulder strains often stem from repetitive overhead shots or improper technique. Wrist injuries can occur from the impact of the ball on the paddle, especially if the wrist is not in a neutral position. Understanding these common issues is the first step in preventing them, ensuring your time on the court is enjoyable and safe.

Preventing such injuries starts with proper warm-up routines and correct playing techniques. A comprehensive warm-up prepares your body for the physical exertion of pickleball, increasing blood flow to the muscles and improving joint mobility. Begin with a general cardiovascular warm-up, such as brisk walking or light jogging, for about 5-10 minutes, followed by dynamic stretches focusing on the legs, arms, and core. These exercises might include leg swings, arm circles, and torso twists, which help reduce muscle stiffness and decrease the risk of injuries. For a detailed guide on integrating these exercises into your routine, refer to the flexibility session in Appendix D.

Incorporating proper techniques into your play is equally crucial. For instance, learning the correct way to perform a serve or a smash can significantly reduce strain on your shoulders and wrists. Work with a coach or an experienced player to ensure your stance and movements are correct. They can provide feedback and adjustments that can make a big difference in how you play and help you avoid common pitfalls that lead to injury.

Using Protective Gear

In terms of equipment, don't underestimate the importance of wearing appropriate footwear. Shoes designed for pickleball, or court sports in general, provide the necessary support and traction to handle quick pivots and lateral movements, reducing the risk of ankle sprains. For players with previous ankle issues, ankle braces or supportive tape can offer additional stability. Knee braces can also be beneficial, especially for players who have experienced knee injuries or chronic knee problems. These braces can help stabilize the knee during the dynamic movements typical of a pickleball game.

Using a wrist brace might help those who have had wrist injuries or are prone to wrist strain. Additionally, consider your paddle's weight and grip size; a paddle that is too heavy or with a grip that is too large or too small can increase the risk of wrist and shoulder injuries. Opt for a paddle that feels comfortable in your hand and balances well with your play style, as this can reduce unnecessary stress on your joints.

Recognizing and Addressing Pain

Listening to your body and recognizing the early signs of potential injury is vital. Common indicators include persistent pain during or after playing, joint swelling, or a decreased range of motion. If you experience any of these symptoms, it's important to take a break from playing and consult a healthcare provider for a proper assessment. Continuing to play through pain can lead to more serious injuries, which might require a longer recovery period.

Rest is a critical component of injury prevention and recovery. Allow adequate recovery time between games, especially if you play frequently or have back-to-back sessions. During rest periods, gentle stretching can help maintain flexibility without putting strain on your muscles and joints. If an injury occurs, follow the RICE method—Rest, Ice, Compression, and Elevation—to manage swelling and initiate the healing process. For more persistent or severe injuries, seeking professional medical advice is essential to receive appropriate treatment and guidance on recovery exercises.

By integrating these preventative practices into your routine, you can enjoy pickleball while minimizing the risk of injury. Remember, the goal is to play smarter and safer, ensuring that each game enhances your health without compromising it. Keep these tips in mind as you step onto the court, and make your well-being as much a priority as your performance.

4.5 Nutrition for Pickleball: Eating for Energy and Recovery

When you're gearing up for a game of pickleball, what you put into your body can be just as important as the physical training you undertake. Nutrition is critical to fuel your body for peak performance and aide in recovery after intense matches. Understanding the basics of a healthy diet tailored for sports can transform how you play and recover, ensuring you're always ready to perform at your best on the court.

A balanced diet for athletes should include a mix of carbohydrates, proteins, and fats, each serving a unique function in body health and athletic performance. Carbohydrates are your body's primary energy source during high-intensity activities like pickleball. They break down into glucose, fueling your muscles and brain during play, and are stored as glycogen in muscles for future energy use. Including various complex carbohydrates in your diet, such as whole grains, fruits, and vegetables, ensures a steady energy release, keeping you powered through long rallies and matches. Foods like oatmeal, whole-grain pasta, and quinoa are excellent sources of complex carbohydrates that provide the sustained energy you need to remain agile and alert.

Proteins are essential for the repair and growth of muscle tissues, which are often stressed during vigorous games. After a match, your muscles need protein to repair micro-tears, which helps them grow stronger over time. Incorporating lean proteins into your diet, such as chicken, turkey, fish, and plant-based sources like beans and lentils, aids in quick recovery, ensuring you're ready for your next game with stronger and more resilient muscles. Combining these proteins with vegetables and healthy fats can enhance muscle recovery and provide additional nutrients that boost overall health.

Recovery nutrition focuses heavily on the period immediately after your play, often referred to as the "golden hour," when muscle sensitivity to nutrients is at its peak. Consuming a mix of proteins and carbohydrates shortly after your matches can significantly enhance your recovery process. A smoothie made with Greek yogurt, fruits, and a handful of spinach offers a quick, nutritious blend of essential proteins and carbohydrates. Additionally, foods rich in omega-3 fatty acids, like salmon or chia seeds, can help reduce inflammation, aiding in faster muscle recovery and reduced soreness.

The timing and frequency of your meals and snacks also play a pivotal role in maintaining optimal energy levels and recovery. Eating a balanced meal about two to three hours before playing ensures you have enough fuel for the game without feeling too full or sluggish. Smaller snacks, like a banana or a small yogurt close to game time, can provide a quick energy boost. After playing, aim to eat within 60 minutes to maximize recovery. Regular, balanced meals throughout the day maintain energy levels and repair muscles more efficiently than sporadic, large meals.

By understanding and implementing these nutritional strategies, you transform your body into a more efficient machine capable of vigorous performance and swift recovery. When managed well, nutrition enhances your physical capabilities and enriches your overall health, allowing you to enjoy every game of pickleball to the fullest. Whether playing a casual afternoon match or competing in a tournament, fueling and refueling your body can make a significant difference in your performance and recovery.

4.6 Hydration Strategies for Long Matches

As you dive deeper into pickleball, understanding hydration's crucial role in enhancing your physical performance and maintaining overall health becomes essential, especially during outdoor or extended matches. Picture this: it's a hot day, you're several games down, and fatigue starts to set in. It's not just the physical exertion that's wearing you down—it's likely a lack of adequate hydration. Keeping your body well-hydrated is akin to ensuring your car has enough oil; it keeps everything running smoothly and prevents the engine—that is, your body—from overheating and breaking down.

The science behind hydration highlights its impact on physical performance. Adequate fluid intake helps maintain blood volume, regulates body temperature, and facilitates muscle contractions. When you're well-hydrated, your heart pumps blood more efficiently, which transports oxygen and essential nutrients to your muscles, keeping them functioning optimally. During a long match, losing just 2% of your body weight in fluid can lead to a noticeable decrease in physical and mental performance. This can mean slower reflexes, reduced accuracy, and a quicker onset of fatigue, all of which can significantly impact your game.

To ensure you're adequately hydrated, follow these specific guidelines: before starting play, aim to drink at least 16-24 ounces of water at least one hour before your game.

This helps start your match well-hydrated. During play, it's recommended to drink 7-10 ounces of water every 10-20 minutes. Post-game, focus on replenishing any fluid lost, drinking 16-24 ounces of water for every pound of body weight lost during the game. This post-game rehydration is crucial for recovery, especially if you're playing multiple matches in a day or over a weekend.

Choosing the right type of fluids is crucial for effective hydration. While water is generally the best way to hydrate, long-duration matches or playing in high temperatures can lead to significant sweat loss, removing water from your body and essential electrolytes like sodium and potassium. These electrolytes help regulate your body's fluid balance and nerve function. In such cases, sipping on an electrolyte-rich sports drink can be beneficial. Sports drinks can replenish lost electrolytes and provide a small amount of energy, thanks to their carbohydrate content, which can be particularly helpful during prolonged play. However, choosing drinks that are low in sugar and artificial additives is important. Coconut water, for example, is a natural alternative that provides electrolytes and hydration without the added sugars found in many commercial sports drinks.

Recognizing and Preventing Dehydration

Recognizing the signs of dehydration can help you take proactive steps to address it before it impacts your performance. Symptoms of dehydration include thirst, reduced sweating, dizziness, fatigue, and dark-colored urine. If you notice these signs, increase your fluid intake immediately. For preventive measures, make a habit of carrying a water bottle during practices and matches, and set reminders to take sips regularly. In environments where you sweat more, such as on hot or humid days, adjust your fluid intake accordingly to counteract the increased fluid loss.

Understanding and implementing effective hydration strategies can transform your play and recovery, ensuring you maintain peak performance throughout your matches. By staying hydrated, you enhance your physical capabilities and ensure a quicker recovery, preparing you for whatever challenge comes next on the court. As you continue to develop your skills and strategies in pickleball, remember that hydration is a key element that supports your overall health and athletic performance, keeping you at the top of your game at all times.

As we wrap up this chapter on physical fitness and nutrition, it's clear that taking care of your body through proper exercise, hydration, and nutrition is as crucial as mastering the skills and strategies of pickleball. Each section of this chapter builds upon the last, forming a comprehensive guide to help you play your best game. Coming up next, we'll explore mental strategies and the psychological aspects of pickleball, which are essential for competing at higher levels and enjoying the game to its fullest. Remember, pickleball isn't just a physical challenge; it's a mental one as well, and preparing your mind is just as important as conditioning your body.

Chapter Five
Mental and Tactical Game

Imagine stepping onto the pickleball court, paddle in hand, heart pounding with anticipation. You see your opponent across the net, ready and waiting. It's not just your physical skills that will lead you to victory; your mental game is equally crucial. How you manage your thoughts and emotions can significantly influence your performance. This chapter explores the psychology of pickleball, helping you harness your mental prowess to complement your physical skills, ensuring you're as sharp mentally as you are physically.

5.1 The Psychology of Pickleball: Winning the Mental Game

Understanding the mental components of pickleball is essential. Confidence, anxiety, and motivation are not just abstract concepts; they are tangible forces that can dictate the pace and outcome of a game. Confidence propels you forward, anxiety can hold you back, and motivation fuels your drive to improve and succeed. Each mental state has a profound effect on how you perform physically. For instance, confidence can enhance your agility and reaction time, making you more likely to reach a tough shot. Conversely, anxiety might tighten your muscles and cloud your decision-making, leading to errors and missed opportunities.

Building mental resilience is a cornerstone of developing a strong mental game. Resilience allows you to bounce back from setbacks and maintain focus and energy, regardless of the score or situation. One effective strategy for building resilience is setting realistic, achievable goals for each match or practice session. Whether it's improving your serve accuracy or mastering a new dinking strategy, having clear objectives can provide a sense of direction and purpose. Maintaining a positive mindset is crucial; focus on what you can control, such as your effort and attitude, rather than external factors like the wind or a noisy crowd. Learning from losses rather than dwelling on them transforms challenges into opportunities for growth, empowering you to refine your strategies and enhance your skills.

Managing emotions on the court is another critical skill. Intense emotions, whether positive or negative, can significantly impact your gameplay. Managing these emotions includes breathing exercises to maintain calm, using positive self-talk to boost your morale, and establishing pre-point routines that help you reset and refocus between rallies. Recognizing the signs of emotional overwhelm early on, such as frustration or overexcitement, allows you to address them promptly, keeping your emotions in check and your mind focused on the game.

Visualization techniques offer a powerful tool to enhance your mental preparation. Visualization involves creating a detailed mental image of successful gameplay, which can improve your confidence and readiness. Before a match, take a few moments to close your eyes and imagine yourself executing perfect shots, moving effortlessly across the court, and responding calmly to your opponent's plays. This mental rehearsal primes your brain to replicate these positive outcomes during actual play, enhancing your performance and decision-making.

Visualization Exercise

Try this simple visualization exercise to boost your game-day performance: Close your eyes and imagine walking onto your favorite pickleball court. Feel the grip of your paddle in your hand and hear the ball popping off the paddle. See yourself serving with precision, the ball landing exactly where you intended. Visualize a challenging rally where you stay calm and focused, moving fluidly and placing your shots perfectly. End the visualization with the joy of winning a point, allowing the feeling of success to fill you up. Regular practice of this exercise can enhance your mental clarity and game-day readiness.

Understanding and applying these psychological principles can elevate your pickleball game to new heights. Integrating mental training into your practice routine is as important as physical training. As you continue to develop your mental game, you'll become a better player and enjoy the sport more, regardless of the pressures of competition. Embrace these mental strategies, practice them diligently, and watch as your confidence and performance soar.

5.2 Concentration Techniques: Staying Focused During Play

In the fast-paced environment of a pickleball game, your ability to concentrate consistently can be just as critical as your physical skills. From the initial serve to the final point, maintaining a laser-sharp focus allows you to respond more effectively to the game's dynamics and keeps you one step ahead of your opponent. Let's explore some practical strategies to enhance your concentration, ensuring that your mental acuity is as honed as your backhand or your serve.

Minimizing distractions is the first step in enhancing your concentration. External distractions can range from unexpected noises from the sidelines to varying weather conditions, while internal pressures might include performance anxiety or overthinking your technique. To manage these effectively, begin by controlling what you can. This might mean choosing quieter courts for practice sessions or wearing a cap to shield your eyes from the sun. A simple yet effective method for internal pressures is to develop a routine that helps anchor your focus. This could include listening to specific music before a game or following a particular warm-up routine that helps you transition into a state of concentration. Over time, these rituals become cues that tell your mind it's time to focus exclusively on the game.

Focus drills are invaluable tools in enhancing your concentration. One effective drill involves timed reaction exercises where you respond to random feeds from a ball machine or a partner. Set a timer and challenge yourself to handle as many randomized shots as possible within the set duration. This drill sharpens your reflexes and trains your brain to maintain focus under time pressure, mimicking match conditions. Another drill is to play practice games where you must remember and execute complex shot sequences. This tests your physical ability to make the shots and challenges your mental capacity to recall and execute under pressure, enhancing your overall game concentration.

Breathing Techniques for Focus

Breathing exercises are another cornerstone of maintaining focus, especially in high-pressure scenarios. Deep, controlled breathing can be a powerful tool for maintaining calm and keeping your mind centered on the present moment. Try incorporating diaphragmatic breathing into your pre-game and in-game routine. This involves breathing deeply into your belly, allowing your diaphragm to expand and your chest to rise slightly. Such breathing helps reduce the physical symptoms of stress, such as elevated heart rate and tense muscles and encourages mental calmness. A simple method to integrate this is to take a few deep breaths before serving or returning, using the rhythm of your breath to anchor your focus.

Sustaining attention throughout a long match tests not just your physical endurance but also your mental stamina. It's natural for concentration to ebb and flow, but the key is to regain focus quickly after distractions or errors. One technique is to use focal points during the game. Whenever your concentration wanes, bring your focus back to a specific physical object—the ball, a line on the court, or even the weave of the net. This refocusing technique is a mental reset, returning your attention to the game. Additionally, between points, instead of dwelling on previous plays, reset your focus by visualizing your next move and planning your strategy one point at a time. This keeps your mind engaged and actively involved in the game, reducing the room for distractions.

By integrating these concentration techniques into your practice and gameplay, you enhance your ability to focus and your overall performance on the court. Remember, concentration is a skill like any physical technique in pickleball—it can be developed and refined over time through consistent practice. So next time you step onto the court, take a moment to center yourself, breathe deeply, and embrace the challenge of maintaining sharp focus, ready to handle whatever the game throws your way.

5.3 Handling Pressure: Tips Tournament Play

When you step onto the court for a tournament, the atmosphere can feel markedly different from your regular practice sessions or friendly matches. The stakes are higher, the audience is larger, and every point feels magnified. Feeling a flutter of nerves is natural, but how you handle this pressure can define your performance. Embracing thorough physical and mental preparation is your first line of defense against the jitters that can accompany competitive play. It's about more than just practicing your swings and serves; it involves preparing your mind to stay calm and focused, no matter the scoreboard.

Preparation for competitive play starts well before the actual tournament. It encompasses everything from ensuring your equipment is in top condition to strategizing about the opponents you may face. However, one often overlooked aspect is the mental rehearsal. Spend time visualizing different match scenarios, including those where you are behind, and imagine yourself playing with composure and precision. This sort of mental prep can be as crucial as physical training, setting a tone of self-assurance that carries you through the day.

Developing coping mechanisms for in-game pressure is also vital. One effective strategy is to focus solely on the point you are playing. This single-point focus helps keep the mind from wandering to the scoreboard or to thoughts of past mistakes. Another technique is establishing a set of cue words anchoring your focus. These can be simple reminders like "smooth" or "steady," helping to center your thoughts and maintain a calm demeanor during play. These cues act as mental resets, keeping your mind aligned with your game strategy.

Experience plays a significant role in managing pressure. Each tournament adds to your reservoir of experiences, teaching you more about your responses to different pressures and competitive environments. These experiences are invaluable; they are real-time lessons that no practice session can fully replicate. Embrace each competitive opportunity, not just as a chance to win but as a chance to learn and grow as a player. Over time, you'll find that situations that once spiked your anxiety become familiar, even manageable. This familiarity breeds confidence, reducing the impact of nerves on your performance.

Post-game reflection is an essential part of learning from each competitive experience. After a tournament, take the time to reflect on your performance. What strategies worked well? What could you have handled better? This isn't about critiquing your performance harshly but rather about understanding it. Keeping a game journal can be a helpful tool in this process. Documenting your thoughts and feelings about each match provides a historical record that you can refer back to, helping you see patterns in your play and emotional responses that you might want to strengthen or improve.

Through these practices, you build not just your skills with the paddle but also your mental toughness, transforming pressure into another component of the game you are well-equipped to handle. As you continue to compete, remember that each match, point, and moment of pressure is shaping you into a more seasoned player who can stand on the court with not just talent but true grit. So, lace up your shoes, grip your paddle, and step onto the court with a mindset that is as prepared and focused as it is excited for the challenge ahead.

5.4 Tactical Shot Selection: Making Smart Decisions

The art of tactical shot selection in pickleball is akin to a chess game; each move on the court should be thoughtfully considered, predicting potential outcomes and always thinking several steps ahead. As you develop your skills in pickleball, understanding how to analyze the game situation quickly becomes crucial. This includes assessing where your opponent is positioned, their strengths and weaknesses, and even their current state of fatigue or frustration. Every shot you choose should be based on a clear understanding of these elements, aimed at exploiting weaknesses or reinforcing your strategic position in the game.

When you're in the midst of a rally, try to gauge your opponent's positioning and readiness quickly. Are they leaning towards one side? Do they look prepared to sprint forward for a drop shot? These observations will guide your shot choices. For instance, if you notice your opponent is far back and struggling with mobility, a well-placed drop shot might be the perfect choice to win the point. Conversely, if they are up close to the net and you find yourself at the baseline, a deep lob can push them back, opening the court for more strategic play. The key is to make these assessments quickly and accurately, turning observations into effective gameplay.

Strategic shot planning extends beyond reacting to your opponent's positioning. It involves setting up the court to your advantage with each shot you make. Think of this as strategic positioning—each shot should aim for immediate gain and consider setting up advantageous positions for subsequent plays. This might mean using a series of shots to maneuver your opponent out of position, creating a vulnerability you can exploit with a decisive power drive or a sneaky sideline shot. Planning your shots in sequences rather than as isolated actions requires a deep understanding of pickleball strategies and the ability to think ahead, predicting both your opponent's movements and the most likely outcomes of each exchange.

The concept of risk versus reward is ever-present in pickleball shot selection. Every shot carries a degree of risk, and part of your development as a player involves understanding when to take these risks. Safe shots might maintain the status quo in the game, but a high-risk, high-reward shot can occasionally be the key to breaking a stalemate or clinching a crucial point. Assessing this risk involves understanding the shot itself and considering the current score, your confidence in making the shot, and the potential impact on the game's momentum. For example, attempting a difficult smash might be worth the risk if you're behind and need to shift the game's momentum. However, if the score is close and the match is at a critical juncture, opting for a safer, more reliable shot might be the wise choice.

Adapting tactics mid-game is crucial in responding to the dynamic nature of pickleball. No game plan survives unchanged in the face of an unpredictable and skilled opponent. You must be willing to adjust your strategies based on the effectiveness of your previous shot selections and the evolving dynamics of the match. This might mean switching from an aggressive, offensive strategy to a more defensive, play-conserving approach if you find yourself leading and wanting to protect that lead. Alternatively, if certain shots or strategies are consistently failing, it's essential to recognize this quickly and adapt—perhaps altering your target areas, changing the spin or speed of your shots, or even just taking a moment to reset mentally and physically.

By mastering these aspects of tactical shot selection, you enhance not only your ability to make smart decisions on the fly but also your overall effectiveness as a pickleball player. Each shot you choose is a building block in the game's strategy, and with each decision, you're weaving together a tapestry of tactics that can lead to victory. As you continue to play and practice, keep these principles in mind, always looking to learn and adapt, ensuring that your shot selection remains a powerful tool in your pickleball arsenal.

5.5 Reading Your Opponent: Anticipating Moves and Countering

Developing keen observational skills is essential in pickleball, where the ability to read your opponent can often be the difference between a point won and a point lost. Observing subtle cues such as paddle position, body language, and movement patterns provides invaluable insights into your opponent's next move, allowing you to prepare and respond effectively. For instance, a slight shift in your opponent's foot positioning or a change in grip on the paddle might indicate a forthcoming smash or a sudden drop shot. By staying alert and decoding these signals, you position yourself to react and proactively counter your opponent's strategies.

Predictive play is an advanced skill that builds on observational insights, enabling you to anticipate and counter your opponent's actions before they unfold. This proactive approach involves making educated guesses about your opponent's next moves based on current gameplay patterns and using this knowledge to your advantage. For example, if your opponent prefers to hit deep from the baseline when under pressure, you can anticipate this move and position yourself to make a strong return or a strategic placement that disrupts their rhythm. Similarly, if an opponent consistently struggles with shots to their backhand, directing more plays to that side can exploit this weakness, increasing your chances of controlling the game.

Developing effective counter-strategies requires a deep understanding of common opponent tendencies and adapting gameplay to exploit these patterns. This might involve recognizing when an opponent will likely execute a particular shot and preparing a series of responses. For example, if you know that your opponent tends to lob when pushed to the back of the court, preparing to move quickly and use an overhead smash can turn their defensive play into your offensive gain. Additionally, adapting your play to target an opponent's weaker returns or exploiting their less agile side with quick directional changes can significantly enhance your tactical advantage. These strategies not only improve your game but also keep your opponent guessing, making it harder for them to settle into a comfortable rhythm.

Practice Scenarios for Anticipating Opponent Moves
Creating practice scenarios that mimic common opponent strategies can greatly enhance your anticipatory skills. Set up drills that simulate different styles of play—such

as aggressive baseline hitting or frequent net play—to familiarize yourself with various strategies and develop appropriate counters. For instance, practice returning smashes with precision or work on your **soft game** to counter powerful hitters. You can also engage in mock games where a coach or partner mimics a known opponent's playing style or creates a playing style, allowing you to practice reading different game patterns and testing out your counter-moves in a controlled environment. These tailored practice sessions improve your ability to read and anticipate and enhance your adaptability, a key component in maintaining a competitive edge regardless of your opponent's style.

By honing these skills and integrating them into your gameplay, you transform your ability to not just play pickleball but also play it with a strategic depth that challenges and outmaneuvers your opponents. Keep practicing, stay observant, and continuously refine your strategies. As you become more adept at reading your opponents and anticipating their moves, you'll find yourself not only keeping up but staying ahead, ready to counter whatever comes your way with confidence and tactical intelligence.

5.6 The Importance of Routine: Pre-Game Preparation

Stepping onto the pickleball court with a clear mind and a focused demeanor starts long before the first serve. It begins with a pre-game routine, a series of actions that set the stage for peak performance. Like a musician tuning their instrument before a concert, a well-honed pre-game routine tunes your body and mind, ensuring you're ready to play your best. This routine encompasses everything from mental warm-ups and physical stretching to a strategic review of your game plan.

Developing a personalized pre-game routine is essential. It should be a tailored set of activities that help you transition into the competitive mindset required for pickleball. For some, this might involve listening to energizing music or engaging in light, dynamic stretches that wake up the muscles. Others might find a few minutes of quiet meditation or visualization more effective. These mental warm-ups can include visualizing successful plays or mentally rehearsing your responses to different game situations, which primes your mind for strategic thinking and focus.

Consistency in your pre-game preparation is vital. The goal is to create a set of rituals that, over time, signal to your brain that it's game time. This consistency helps reduce anxiety and increases confidence because it becomes a familiar process that reliably prepares you for performance. Whether it's a morning match or an evening game, whether you feel at the top of your game or slightly off, adhering to your routine can provide a sense of normalcy and control. It's about creating a predictable environment that breeds confidence, no matter the external conditions.

Tailoring your routine to fit your specific needs and the day's conditions is another layer of strategic preparation. Consider the time of day your match is scheduled. Morning games might require a longer warm-up to shake off the stiffness from sleep, while afternoon games might need a focus on hydration and maintaining energy levels. Similarly, adapt your routine based on your physical condition. If you're feeling tight, incorporate additional stretching or a longer warm-up. If you're nervous, spend more time on mental exercises to calm your mind. This adaptability ensures that your preparation meets your needs precisely, allowing you to enter each game in your best possible state.

Role of Rituals in Pre-Game Routines

Incorporating small personal rituals into your pre-game routine also carries significant psychological benefits. These rituals, whether wearing a particular article of clothing, performing a specific sequence of stretches, or reciting a personal mantra, can serve as powerful psychological anchors. They provide comfort and build a mental and emotional fortress around you, shielding you from pressure and distractions. For instance, a player might always tie their shoelaces in a particular pattern before a game, or another might tap their paddle against their shoes three times before stepping onto the court. These seemingly insignificant rituals can significantly boost confidence and provide a psychological edge.

As you develop and refine your pre-game routine, remember that its ultimate goal is to put you in the best frame of mind and physical readiness for the game. It's a personalized process that, when done consistently, becomes a cornerstone of your competitive play. By taking the time to understand what works best for you and being willing to adapt and refine your routine over time, you set yourself up for success on the court.

Embrace the power of a well-crafted pre-game routine. Let it be your secret weapon that consistently brings out your best game regardless of the opponent or the stakes of the match. This preparation is not just about getting ready for a match; it's about respecting the sport and honoring your commitment to playing your best, one game at a time. As we transition from focusing on individual preparation to exploring the broader dynamics of pickleball strategy in the next chapter, carry forward the discipline and mindfulness that a solid pre-game routine develops. It's these qualities that will not only enhance your performance but also enrich your overall experience with the sport.

Chapter Six
The Social Aspect of Pickleball

6.1 Finding and Joining Pickleball Clubs and Leagues

IMAGINE STEPPING ONTO THE court where the air buzzes with the pop of pickleball paddles and the warmth of shared laughter and camaraderie. Joining a pickleball club or league can transform the game from a simple activity into a rich social experience, creating opportunities for friendship and competition alike. Whether you're just starting out or looking to sharpen your skills in a more structured setting, finding the right club or league is a pivotal step.

Researching Local Options

The first step in your quest to find the ideal pickleball community is research. Start with your local community centers and parks. Many offer regular pickleball sessions and can connect you with local groups. Additionally, the internet is a treasure trove of information. Websites dedicated to pickleball, such as USA Pickleball, provide directories of local clubs and leagues. These resources often include contact information, meeting times, and locations, making finding a group that matches your schedule and interests easier.

Social media platforms can also be invaluable in this search. Look for Facebook groups or Meetup events centered around pickleball in your area. These groups often post updates about upcoming games or events, providing a real-time peek into the community's vibe and activity level. Engaging with these online communities can also give you a sense of the group's social dynamics before you even set foot on the court.

Evaluating the Right Fit

Once you've located a few potential clubs or leagues, consider what you're looking to gain from the experience. If you're new to the game, you might prefer a club with a strong focus on instruction and skill development, possibly one that offers coaching sessions or beginner clinics. On the other hand, if competition is what drives you, look for leagues that organize regular tournaments or competitive play sessions.

Location is also a crucial factor—picking a club that's easy to reach increases the likelihood that you'll attend regularly. Additionally, visit the venues if possible. This visit can provide insight into the facilities' quality and whether they are well-maintained, which can greatly affect your playing experience.

Membership Benefits

Joining a pickleball club or league comes with a plethora of benefits. Regular play sessions in a structured environment can improve your skills faster than casual play. Many clubs also offer structured training programs or clinics that can provide personalized guidance to refine your technique.

Moreover, being part of a club often gives you access to sanctioned tournaments. These events are not just about displaying your skills but also about testing them against a broader spectrum of players, which is invaluable for your growth in the sport. Additionally, many clubs negotiate discounts on equipment and court fees for their members, which can make playing pickleball more affordable.

First Steps to Joining

Ready to take the plunge? Here's how you can start:

1. <u>Reach Out</u>: Once you've chosen a club or league, the next step is to make contact. Send an email or make a call. Introduce yourself, express your interest in joining, and ask about the process. This initial interaction can also give you a sense of how welcoming and responsive the community is.

2. <u>Visit a Session</u>: Many clubs are happy to let potential members visit a session or play a trial game. This visit can be crucial in deciding if the club's atmosphere and level of play are right for you.

3. <u>Apply for Membership</u>: If your visit goes well and you decide to join, the next step is to apply for membership. This process might involve filling out a form and paying membership dues. Ensure you understand what your membership entails and any responsibilities you might have as a member.

4. <u>Attend Regularly</u>: Once you've joined, make the most of your membership by participating in sessions and events. Regular attendance helps improve your game and solidifies your place within the community.

By following these steps, you can find a pickleball club or league that helps you enjoy the game more and enriches your social life, connecting you with like-minded individuals who share your passion for this fast-growing sport. Whether you want to make new friends, improve your game, or simply have fun, the pickleball community welcomes you with open arms. So, grab your paddle, step out onto the court, and get ready to enjoy the social whirl of pickleball like never before.

6.2 The Etiquette of Pickleball: Rules of Conduct

When you step onto a pickleball court, it's not just about swinging paddles and hitting balls; it's about engaging with a community that values respect, sportsmanship, and mutual enjoyment of the game. Understanding and adhering to pickleball etiquette ensures that everyone, from beginners to seasoned players, can enjoy the sport in a friendly and safe environment. Let's explore some fundamental aspects of pickleball etiquette that help maintain this positive atmosphere.

Basic Court Courtesy

Court courtesy is essential and starts with simple behaviors that show respect for other players and the facilities. One basic rule is to avoid walking behind a court while a game is in progress. This helps minimize distractions for the players and shows respect for their game. Additionally, keeping noise to a minimum, especially during rallies, is a courtesy all players appreciate. This includes moderating voices and avoiding unnecessary noise, such as from paddle banging or loud celebrations, which can disrupt the concentration and enjoyment of others.

Respecting the lines and calls of other players is also crucial. In pickleball, players often make their own line calls unless playing in a game with line judges. This self-officiating aspect of the game relies heavily on player integrity and respect for one another. Always give your opponents the benefit of the doubt in close calls; losing a point in good spirit is better than winning one amid contention.

Handling Disputes

No matter how careful you are, disputes can still arise, whether over scoring, line calls, or player conduct. Handling these disputes gracefully is key to maintaining a positive environment. If there's a disagreement, the first step is to discuss it calmly and openly, trying to see the situation from your opponent's perspective. Often, a simple, respectful conversation can resolve misunderstandings.

If the dispute involves rules or scoring and cannot be resolved through discussion, it may be helpful to consult a third party, such as a club official or a more experienced player, for clarification. Remember, the goal of resolving disputes is not just to determine who is right but to continue the game in a spirit of fairness and enjoyment. Always prioritize the health of relationships over the competitiveness of the game.

Sportsmanship

Sportsmanship is perhaps the most cherished aspect of pickleball etiquette. It involves showing respect for your opponents, the officials, and the rules of the game, regardless of the outcome. This respect is demonstrated in actions like shaking hands or offering a friendly word after a game, celebrating points without gloating, and giving sincere compliments for good plays. Encouraging less experienced players is also part of good sportsmanship; it fosters a supportive environment that enhances everyone's experience and growth in the sport.

Supporting your fellow players in victory and defeat strengthens the community and enhances everyone's enjoyment of the game. Remember, pickleball is as much about the people you meet and the friendships you form as it is about the points you score.

Joining Open Play and Navigating Player Levels

In open play at a pickleball club or outdoor court, there is often a system for players to rotate into games. The general etiquette is to place your paddle in line or in a designated area, indicating that you are waiting to join the next available game. When it's your turn, the players who have been on the court the longest typically rotate off to allow new players to step in. However, this can vary depending on the group or venue, so it's helpful to observe how others are handling rotation or to ask someone familiar with the court's routine.

For new or advanced beginner players, joining a game with intermediate or more experienced players can be a bit daunting. It's generally okay to politely ask if you can join a game, especially during open play. Most pickleball communities are welcoming, and players will often be happy to include you, though some games may have skill-level preferences. When joining an intermediate game, it's courteous to be flexible about your positioning on the court. Traditionally, the weaker player is placed on the right side to receive serves, but this is not a strict rule. You may find that more experienced players will guide you on positioning during the game.

Remember, open play is as much about fun and learning as it is about competition. Don't hesitate to ask questions or for tips, and be mindful of the pace and expectations of the group. The key is to show respect, be willing to learn, and enjoy the shared experience on the court.

Safety Norms

Safety is paramount in pickleball, not just for your well-being but for everyone on the court. Adhering to safety norms helps prevent accidents and ensures the game is enjoyable. This includes using proper equipment, like shoes that provide adequate support and grip, and using balls that are appropriate for the playing environment (indoor or outdoor).

Be mindful of your and others' physical condition. If you or another player is feeling unwell or is injured, it's wise to pause the game and seek the necessary care. Also, be aware of the space around you to avoid collisions, especially in doubles play. Communicate clearly with your partner about who will take the ball to avoid accidental paddle clashes or falls.

Following these etiquette guidelines contributes to a respectful, enjoyable, and safe playing environment. This makes the game more enjoyable and deepens your connections within the pickleball community, making every match an opportunity to foster goodwill and lasting friendships. Remember, the true spirit of pickleball lies in the joy of the game and the respect shared among its players. So, the next time you step onto the court, bring your paddle and your best display of etiquette and watch as the game unfolds in the most enjoyable way possible.

6.3 Organizing and Participating in Pickleball Events

Organizing a pickleball event, whether a cozy gathering for local club members or a large-scale tournament, is not just about setting up nets and marking lines—it's about creating an atmosphere where passion for the game can flourish, and participants can engage in healthy competition and camaraderie. The process begins with a clear understanding of the event's scope and objectives. Are you aiming to foster community engagement, offer competitive play, or perhaps raise funds for a good cause? Clarifying your goals early on will guide every decision, from the format of the games to the choice of venue.

Event Planning Basics

The first step in planning your pickleball event is selecting the right date and venue. Consider a date that avoids major holidays or community events that might affect turnout. When choosing a venue, ensure it has adequate courts to accommodate your expected number of participants, plus some extra space for spectators and resting players. It's also crucial to check that the venue has proper facilities such as restrooms, drinking water, and first aid amenities, which are essential for participant comfort and safety.

Once the logistics are squared away, it's time to think about the format of the pickleball event. Will it be a tournament with structured brackets or a more relaxed round-robin where everyone gets to play multiple games? Each format has its benefits and can be tailored to the goals of your event. For tournaments, consider how you'll handle registrations, match scheduling, and scoring. Tools like online registration platforms can streamline participant sign-ups and fee collection, while digital apps for brackets and scoring can keep the event running smoothly on the day.

Roles and Responsibilities

A clear definition of roles and responsibilities is crucial for the smooth execution of any event. As the organizer, you'll need a reliable team whose members understand their tasks and are committed to the event's success. Key roles might include a tournament director, who oversees all aspects of gameplay; volunteers who manage registration tables and scorekeeping; and facilities coordinators who ensure the venue is prepared and maintained throughout the event.

It's also beneficial to assign roles for handling food and beverages, especially if your event spans a whole day. Participants and spectators will appreciate having access to snacks and drinks, and this aspect of the event can also be an opportunity for additional fundraising through sales.

Promoting Events

Effective promotion is key to ensuring your pickleball event attracts participants and spectators. Start by creating eye-catching flyers and posters to distribute in local community centers, gyms, and sports stores. Utilize social media platforms to reach a broader audience—regular posts leading up to the event can generate excitement and encourage sign-ups. Consider creating an event page on Facebook where participants can get updates, ask questions, and interact with each other before the event.

Engaging local media is another powerful tool for event promotion. A small piece in the local newspaper or a mention on a community radio station can significantly boost your event's visibility. Don't underestimate the power of personal invitations either; sometimes, a direct invitation can be more effective than broader advertising efforts.

Hosting Inclusive Events

Inclusivity should be a cornerstone of any pickleball event. Aim to create an environment where players of all ages, skill levels, and backgrounds feel welcome and valued. This can be achieved by offering different categories or divisions in the tournament, such as beginner, intermediate, and advanced, or having specific matches for youth and senior players.

Consider also the accessibility of your event. Ensure that the venue is accessible to people with disabilities and have staff available to assist participants or spectators who might need additional help. Offering equipment like lighter paddles or adaptive seating can also make a big difference in making everyone feel included.

Creating a positive, inclusive atmosphere extends beyond physical accommodations. It's about fostering a spirit of respect and encouragement among all participants. Encourage experienced players to support beginners, perhaps even organizing a short workshop or warm-up session before the main event where new players can learn basic skills and rules. This not only improves their game experience but also strengthens the community bonds that pickleball is known for.

By carefully planning and promoting your pickleball event and ensuring it is inclusive and welcoming, you contribute to the sport's growth and enhance the social fabric of your community. Each event is an opportunity to celebrate this dynamic sport and the diverse community of players it attracts. So, take the leap, organize with care, and watch as your pickleball event becomes a highlight in your community's sporting calendar, bringing people together in exciting, enjoyable competition and friendship.

6.4 Building a Pickleball Network: Tips for Social Success

Navigating the social landscape of pickleball can be as thrilling as the game itself. Building a robust network within this community enhances your enjoyment of the sport and opens doors to new opportunities and friendships. Imagine walking onto a court where you're greeted by familiar faces, where every game is a chance to connect and share, not just compete. Achieving this level of social integration involves more than just showing up to play; it requires active engagement and a strategic approach to networking.

Networking Strategies

The pickleball community is diverse, including players of all ages and backgrounds, which makes it a perfect environment for broadening your social circle. Participating in mixers is a fantastic way to meet new people. These events are usually designed to be fun and social, often pairing players randomly or rotating partners throughout the event. This setup encourages you to interact with a variety of players, making it easier to strike up conversations and make new acquaintances.

Attending clinics and workshops offers another avenue for networking. These events not only help you improve your skills but also allow you to connect with others who are eager to learn and grow in the sport. Being in a learning environment fosters a sense of camaraderie as you and your peers tackle new challenges and celebrate progress together.

Volunteering at tournaments and club events is also a highly effective networking strategy. As a volunteer, you interact with a wide array of participants, from organizers and fellow volunteers to players and spectators. This role often puts you at the heart of the event, making it easy to engage with the community and build relationships based on shared experiences and contributions.

Leveraging Social Media

In today's digital age, social media is a powerful tool for connecting with the pickleball community. Platforms like Facebook, Instagram, and Twitter offer numerous groups and pages dedicated to pickleball enthusiasts. By joining these online communities, you can stay informed about local events, share experiences, and participate in discussions. Posting regularly about your pickleball activities, whether it's a photo from a recent game or tournament or a tip you've found helpful, can draw others to you, sparking conversations and connections that extend beyond the digital realm.

YouTube is also a valuable resource for connecting with the broader pickleball community. On this platform, many players and coaches share tutorials, match analyses, and personal pickleball journeys. Engaging with this content by commenting, asking questions, or even sharing your own videos can help you connect with like-minded individuals and become more visible in the community.

Building Lasting Relationships

While making new connections is important, nurturing them into lasting relationships is key to building a strong network. Regular engagement is crucial. This means not only seeing people at games but also reaching out through texts or social media, sharing interesting pickleball articles, or inviting someone for a practice session. Celebrating your contacts' victories and supporting them through challenges related to pickleball or personal life can deepen connections and build mutual trust and respect.

Another aspect of building lasting relationships is reciprocity. Be ready to offer the same level of support and engagement that you seek from others. Whether it's showing up to cheer for a friend during a tournament or offering to help a new player refine their skills, your willingness to contribute to the well-being and success of others will not go unnoticed.

Benefits of a Strong Network

The benefits of a well-established pickleball network are manifold. Socially, it means always having someone to play with, which can be particularly motivating. It helps maintain a regular playing schedule and pushes you to improve your skills. On a personal level, these relationships can enrich your life, providing support and friendship that extend beyond the court.

Professionally, a strong network can open up opportunities within and outside the pickleball world. For those interested in coaching, event organization, or starting a pickleball-related business, having a solid network means access to potential clients, partners, or mentors. Moreover, leadership roles within clubs often go to those who are well-connected and respected within the community, providing a chance to shape the future of the sport locally.

Building a network within the pickleball community is about more than just playing a sport. It's about creating a vibrant, supportive social circle that enhances every aspect of your experience. As you continue to engage with and contribute to this community, remember that every interaction is an opportunity to strengthen connections, enrich your social life, and expand your horizons in the exciting world of pickleball.

6.5 Community Building Through Pickleball

Pickleball isn't just a sport; it's a vibrant community activity that has the power to bring people together, fostering a sense of belonging and mutual respect among its players. Creating a community culture around pickleball goes beyond organizing games and tournaments; it involves cultivating an environment where every participant, regardless of their background or skill level, feels valued and engaged. The ethos of inclusivity and diversity should be at the heart of every club or group, ensuring that everyone, from the enthusiastic beginner to the seasoned pro, feels an integral part of the pickleball family.

One effective way to foster such a culture is through regular community meetings that go beyond discussing backhands and strategies. These gatherings can be used to share experiences, address group challenges, and brainstorm ideas for making the club more welcoming. Consider hosting these sessions in a casual setting, perhaps after a round of games, where members can relax, mingle, and open up more freely. In these informal spaces, barriers break down, and true community spirit is forged. During these gatherings, emphasize the importance of everyone's voice, encouraging suggestions on how the club can better serve its diverse membership base. This could range from adjusting game schedules to better accommodate working members to introducing more family-friendly events that allow everyone to get involved.

Beyond internal community building, pickleball clubs can significantly impact their local communities through outreach projects. Organizing charity tournaments is a fantastic way to give back while enjoying the sport. These events raise funds for worthy causes and bring a sense of purpose and community pride to club members. Another impactful project could be setting up pickleball clinics for youth in the community. These clinics can introduce kids to healthy activities and provide them with valuable lessons in teamwork and sportsmanship. By involving club members in the planning and execution of these projects, you not only aid the community but also enrich the members' experience and commitment to the club.

Engaging with local businesses can provide another layer of community integration. Local businesses can be invaluable allies in growing your pickleball community, from sponsoring events to providing venues or equipment. Start by identifying businesses that align with the health and lifestyle aspects of pickleball, such as sports shops, health food stores, or local gyms. Reach out to them with tailored sponsorship packages that offer mutual benefits. For instance, businesses can display their branding at events while the pickleball club enjoys the benefits of additional resources. Engagements like these provide financial or material support and strengthen the community's economic ecosystem, promoting a symbiotic relationship between the club and local commerce.

The impact of a thriving pickleball community on a local area can be profound. Active sports communities often foster greater social cohesion, bringing together individuals from diverse backgrounds and contributing to a more interconnected community. Economic benefits are also significant. Regular events and tournaments can boost local businesses, from increased foot traffic for nearby shops and restaurants to sponsorship opportunities for larger companies. On a broader scale, an active pickleball community can enhance the local area's appeal, attracting more residents and visitors who are drawn to vibrant, community-focused environments. This not only boosts local economies but also enriches the community's cultural landscape.

As you continue to weave these threads of engagement, diversity, and mutual respect into the fabric of your pickleball community, remember that each element contributes to a richer, more vibrant tapestry. From fostering a welcoming club culture to engaging in community projects and building strong local partnerships, every effort you make enhances the pickleball experience and reinforces the sport's unique ability to bring people together, creating lasting impacts both on and off the court.

6.6 Volunteering and Leadership in the Pickleball Community

Stepping into a role that transcends playing for personal enjoyment and into one where you contribute to the fabric of the pickleball community can be incredibly rewarding.

Volunteering within this vibrant community means not only giving back but also growing personally and professionally. Various opportunities abound, from organizing local tournaments to coaching beginners. Each position offers a unique chance to enhance the structure and spirit of the game, ensuring it thrives at all levels.

One of the most impactful ways you can contribute is by volunteering at community events or local tournaments. These roles often require a range of skills, from logistical planning to effective communication, providing a fertile ground for developing leadership qualities. Alternatively, coaching beginners or running workshops help new players improve their skills and allows you to refine your understanding of the game, communicate effectively, and inspire others. These roles often do not require professional qualifications but rather a passion for the game and a commitment to fostering a supportive environment.

Volunteering also offers a unique platform to develop and showcase leadership skills. Leadership here is about more than guiding a team or managing an event; it's about inspiring enthusiasm, fostering inclusivity, and being proactive in solving problems. For instance, leading a committee to improve local pickleball facilities enhances your project management skills and gives you a tangible way to contribute to the community's growth. These experiences can be instrumental in cultivating skills such as strategic thinking, public speaking, and negotiation, which are invaluable in various aspects of life beyond pickleball.

The satisfaction and recognition that come with volunteering can be profoundly fulfilling. Being acknowledged by your peers for your efforts in organizing a successful tournament or seeing a new player you coached win their first game can provide a sense of accomplishment that transcends the usual joys of the sport. Recognition can also come in more formal forms, such as awards or public acknowledgment at events, which can further cement your role and reputation within the community.

To support volunteers, many pickleball clubs and organizations offer training and resources to help them perform their roles effectively. This might include workshops on event management, seminars on coaching techniques, or even online resources for best practices in club governance. This support not only helps volunteers feel more confident and capable in their roles but also ensures a high standard of leadership and organization within the community.

By choosing to volunteer, you enrich your life and strengthen the pickleball community. Your efforts contribute to a sport that offers joy, health, and connection to so many, amplifying the positive impact of pickleball far beyond the courts. Whether you are keeping score at a tournament, teaching a new player the basics, or leading a local pickleball expansion project, your involvement is a vital part of what makes the pickleball community vibrant and enduring.

As we close this chapter on the social aspects of pickleball, remember that each role you take, each event you help organize, and every new player you welcome into the community enhances your experience and weaves a stronger, more vibrant tapestry of this sport. The connections made, the leadership skills honed, and the joy shared contribute to a richer pickleball culture and a more engaged community. Looking ahead, the next chapter will discuss the technical nuances of pickleball equipment, helping you make informed choices that can enhance your performance and enjoyment of the game. So, keep your paddle ready and your spirit open to the endless possibilities that pickleball offers both on and off the court.

Chapter Seven
Equipment Deep Dive

Picture yourself stepping onto the court with a paddle that feels like a natural extension of your arm. It's perfectly balanced, and every swing connects with the ball just as you intend. This isn't just a dream scenario; understanding the anatomy of your paddle and the materials from which it's made can transform this vision into your reality. In this chapter, we're going to dive deep into pickleball equipment, focusing particularly on paddles—their materials, weight, and how these factors influence your game. By the end of this section, you'll be equipped with the knowledge to choose a paddle that complements your style and elevates your play.

7.1 Paddle Anatomy: Materials, Weight, and Balance

Understanding Paddle Components

A pickleball paddle may seem straightforward at first glance, but it's a complex piece of equipment designed to enhance playability and performance. Let's dissect the paddle, starting with its core, which is the central part of the paddle that provides the main structure. The core can be made from various materials such as polymer, nomex, or aluminum, each affecting the paddle's feel and sound. A polymer core is known for its soft control and is quite popular among players who value precision and a quieter hit. Nomex, a nylon-based material, creates a denser core with more power but with a louder pop, making it ideal for players who prefer a hard-driving game. Aluminum cores strike a balance between power and control and tend to be lighter, which can reduce player fatigue over long matches.

Moving outward from the core, the face of the paddle is what actually contacts the ball, and it can be crafted from composite materials or graphite. Graphite faces are lightweight and stiff, allowing for quick, precise shots. Composite faces are usually made from a blend of fiberglass and resin, offering a good balance of power and control with a larger sweet spot than graphite. This makes composite paddles a versatile choice that is suitable for various playing styles.

The edge guard is the protective rim around the paddle that helps prevent damage from the paddle hitting the ground. While some players opt for edgeless paddles for a larger playing surface, having an edge guard can significantly extend the life of your paddle by protecting it from damage.

Materials Used in Paddle Construction

The choice of materials in paddle construction directly impacts the paddle's durability, playing characteristics, and even the sound it makes upon impact with the ball. As discussed, the core material affects the paddle's overall feel and sound. For instance, paddles with a polymer core tend to be quieter and absorb more shock, which can be easier on your arm. The material of the paddle's face also plays a critical role. Graphite faces provide a stiffer, more responsive surface, allowing for precise shot-making. Composite faces offer more power and a larger sweet spot, which can be forgiving for new players or those who don't always hit the ball squarely.

Importance of Paddle Weight and Balance

The weight of a paddle is pivotal in determining how it feels during play and can affect your reaction speed and stamina. Paddles typically range from 6 to 14 ounces. A lighter paddle (6-7.5 ounces) is easier to maneuver and can be great for players who value speed and finesse over power. Lighter paddles reduce arm fatigue, making them a good choice for players with joint issues or those who play for extended periods. On the other hand, heavier paddles (8 ounces and above) provide more power but can be more taxing on your arm and shoulder, potentially leading to quicker fatigue. Finding a balance that complements your physical capabilities and playing style is crucial.

The balance of a paddle refers to how the weight is distributed. A head-heavy paddle can deliver more power on swings, while a head-light paddle offers better control and is easier to maneuver. Testing different paddles to find one that feels balanced in your hand is key to finding the right fit.

Impact of Paddle Shape and Size

Paddle shape significantly influences play. Traditional paddles are wider with a shorter handle, which provides a larger surface area for hitting but can reduce reach. Elongated paddles have a longer reach and a larger sweet spot, making them ideal for players who play a power game from the baseline. The shape of your paddle should complement your play style; for instance, a wide-body paddle might benefit a player who enjoys playing at the net and needs a larger surface area for blocking shots, while an elongated paddle might suit a baseline player looking for extra reach and power.

Choosing the right paddle involves understanding these elements and how they interact with your unique playing style and physical needs. Whether you're a beginner learning the ropes or an advanced player fine-tuning your game, the right paddle can make a significant difference. By considering the materials, weight, balance, and shape of your paddle, you can select equipment that improves your performance and enhances your overall playing experience. Remember, the best paddle for you is one that feels like an extension of your body, complementing your movements and style of play on the court.

7.2 Choosing the Right Paddle for Your Style of Play

Every pickleball player brings their unique flair and strategy to the court, whether you're a power player who dominates with forceful shots, a finesse player who masters the art of placement, or perhaps you blend both styles into your gameplay. Understanding your personal playing style is the first step in choosing a paddle that enhances your strengths and helps compensate for any weaknesses. For the power player, a heavier paddle with a polymer core might be ideal, providing the additional weight needed to drive the ball across the court. On the other hand, finesse players might prefer a lighter composite paddle that offers better control and a softer touch, perfect for those precise shots just over the net. If you find yourself somewhere in the middle, experimenting with a mid-weight paddle that offers a good balance of power and control could be the way to go.

Selecting the right paddle isn't just about how you play the game; it's also about ensuring it fits comfortably in your hand. The grip size of a paddle is critical because it impacts your ability to swing the paddle effectively and without strain. A grip that's too large can lead to a lack of control and increased fatigue, while a grip that's too small can cause unnecessary wrist action, which might lead to injury over time. To find your ideal grip size, you can measure from the middle crease of your palm to the tip of your ring finger. This measurement typically ranges between four and five inches, corresponding to the circumference of the paddle's handle. Many players find that adding an overgrip to the handle can also provide additional comfort, absorb sweat, and customize the feel to better suit their hand.

Now, when it comes to testing paddles, think of it like choosing a dance partner—it has to be a good fit for your style to perform your best. Before making a purchase, it's wise to test various paddles under different playing conditions. Many sports shops and clubs offer demo programs where you can try out different paddles during a game or in the shop. Pay attention to how each paddle feels in terms of weight, balance, and grip. Does it enhance your swing speed? Do you feel like you have to work harder to achieve the shots you want? How does it handle soft shots compared to powerful drives? Testing in various conditions, such as indoor versus outdoor play, can also influence your decision. Factors like wind and temperature can affect paddle performance, and what works well in a calm, indoor environment may not hold up in an outdoor setting with natural elements at play.

For players at different skill levels, the choice of paddle can significantly influence your development and enjoyment of the game. Beginners might benefit from a lighter, wider paddle that offers a larger surface area and reduces the chance of missing the ball. Such paddles often provide a good balance of control and power, allowing new players to learn the ropes without feeling overwhelmed by a paddle that is too specialized. Intermediate players might start to look for a paddle that complements their developing style, whether leaning towards power or control. At this stage, experimenting with different materials and weights can help refine your skills and prepare you for more competitive play.

Advanced players typically have a very good understanding of their needs and how their paddle choice affects their performance. They might opt for high-end models offering the latest technology and materials, such as carbon fiber faces or specialized cores designed to enhance spin and control.

By carefully considering how a paddle aligns with your playing style, comfort, and skill level, you can make an informed choice that not only boosts your performance but also increases your enjoyment of the game. Remember, the right paddle feels like an extension of your arm, perfectly suited to your approach to the game. Whether you're just starting out or have been playing for years, selecting the right paddle can make all the difference in your pickleball experience.

7.3 Ball Varieties: Indoor vs. Outdoor

When stepping onto the pickleball court, whether it's nestled in a cozy indoor setting or basking under the open sky, the choice of ball can significantly influence your gameplay. Let's look at the differences between indoor and outdoor pickleball balls, not only in their physical characteristics but also in how they interact with various playing environments. Understanding these nuances will help you select the perfect ball that enhances your performance and enjoyment, no matter where your games take place.

Differences in Ball Construction

Indoor and outdoor pickleball balls may look similar at first glance, but their differences become quite clear upon closer inspection. Indoor balls, for instance, typically have 26 larger holes, which contribute to their slower travel through the air—ideal for the controlled environment of indoor courts. The larger hole diameter and lighter weight make these balls softer, providing a tactile feel that favors strategic play with a focus on precision.

On the other hand, outdoor pickleball balls are designed to tackle the challenges of playing outside. These balls generally have 40 smaller holes, allowing them to better handle windy conditions by maintaining a consistent flight path. The increased number of holes also aids in controlling the ball's movement despite external elements like wind. Outdoor balls are made from harder plastic, making them heavier and more durable against the rough surfaces of outdoor courts. However, this increased hardness means that outdoor balls, while durable, tend to crack more quickly than their softer indoor counterparts. Whether you're facing wind or sun, outdoor pickleballs are built to provide consistent performance in the more unpredictable outdoor environment.

Choosing the Right Ball for the Environment

Selecting the right ball type is crucial and can be influenced by factors beyond just whether you are indoors or outdoors. Consider the type of court and its surface. For instance, if playing outdoors on a rough concrete surface, an outdoor ball's durability and design will likely offer better playability and resistance to wear while providing consistent bounce and flight characteristics. On the other hand, if playing indoors on a wooden surface, an indoor ball will likely perform better, as its softer design complements the smoother, faster surface of the court.

However, there may be instances where you might choose to use an indoor ball for outdoor play or an outdoor ball indoors. For example, if you're playing outside on a calm day and prefer a slower, more controlled game, an indoor ball might be a good choice. Its lighter weight and larger holes make it travel more slowly through the air, emphasizing strategy and precision. This can be particularly beneficial for beginners or players looking to practice finesse shots without the interference of wind.

Conversely, opting for an outdoor ball could be advantageous if you're playing indoors but want to increase the game's pace. The heavier, harder construction of outdoor balls results in faster play and a higher bounce, challenging your reflexes and quick decision-making. Additionally, on particularly slick indoor surfaces, the outdoor ball's smaller holes and greater weight can help maintain a more predictable flight path, offering better control for experienced players.

Ultimately, the choice of ball can significantly influence your playing style. If you enjoy a fast-paced, power-driven game, the sturdier outdoor ball can complement your style, especially in breezy conditions where a heavier ball provides more control. Conversely, if your strategy relies more on finesse and precision, the indoor ball, with its slower speed and increased control, might be your ally, helping you execute meticulous shots with greater ease.

Impact of Weather and Temperature

Environmental factors like wind and temperature can significantly affect how a pickleball behaves during play. Outdoor balls are designed to perform well in various weather conditions; however, even these balls can be influenced by extreme temperatures. In colder weather, the ball becomes harder and less responsive, which can affect both the bounce and the feel of the ball during play. Conversely, the ball can soften in warmer temperatures, which may increase its bounce and speed. Adjusting your playing style to these conditions is crucial. For example, in cold weather, you might need to hit harder to get the same response from the ball, whereas in hot conditions, a softer touch may be necessary to maintain control.

Maintenance and Lifespan of Balls

Maintaining the quality of your pickleball balls is essential for ensuring optimal performance during play. Regular inspection of the balls for cracks, unusual wear, or deformation is key. An indoor ball might show signs of softening or loss of texture, which can alter its performance characteristics, while an outdoor ball might become rough or develop small cracks that could affect its flight path. Replacing your balls at the first sign of significant wear is important to maintain the quality of your game.

Proper storage of balls also contributes to their lifespan and performance. Keep them in a cool, dry place away from direct sunlight, as UV rays and heat can degrade the plastic used in pickleball balls, leading to premature aging. Avoid leaving balls in your car or in outdoor locations where they can be exposed to the elements for prolonged periods.

By understanding the distinctions between indoor and outdoor pickleball balls and how to choose and care for them based on your environment, you can significantly enhance both your performance and enjoyment of the game. Whether you are playing a casual game with friends or competing in a tournament, the right ball can make all the difference.

7.4 Apparel and Accessories for Every Player

Stepping onto the pickleball court isn't just about having the right paddle and ball; it's also about dressing for success. How you dress can significantly affect your comfort and performance during a game. The right apparel does more than just make you look good; it supports your body's needs during intense play, helping you to move freely and stay focused. Moisture-wicking fabrics are a game-changer in sports apparel, especially in a fast-paced game like pickleball. These materials draw sweat away from your body to the fabric's surface, where it evaporates, keeping you dry and comfortable during play. This feature can be particularly beneficial on hot days or during intense matches when staying cool and dry is crucial to maintaining your performance. Additionally, the fit of your clothing should allow for a full range of motion. Look for form-fitting yet flexible items that allow you to move naturally and without restriction. Clothes that are too tight can inhibit movement and even affect your circulation, while baggy clothes can catch on your paddle or get in the way during play.

Footwear for Safety and Performance

The importance of proper footwear cannot be overstated when it comes to playing pickleball. Your shoes are your foundation, and they need to provide both support and flexibility to help you move quickly and safely around the court. When choosing shoes for pickleball, look for models designed specifically for court sports, as they offer the necessary lateral support needed to handle quick changes in direction. Cushioning is another important feature, as it absorbs the impact each time your foot hits the ground, reducing stress on your ankles and knees. The tread pattern on the sole of the shoe also matters; it should provide sufficient grip to prevent slipping but not so much that it catches on the court surface and impedes movement. Each of these factors plays a crucial role in enhancing your performance and preventing injuries during play.

Essential Accessories

Beyond clothing and shoes, several accessories can enhance your pickleball-playing experience. Hats and sunglasses are crucial for outdoor play; they protect your eyes from the sun and improve visibility. Look for sunglasses with polarized lenses to reduce glare, which can be a serious hindrance on sunny days. Sweatbands, worn on the wrist and forehead, can also improve comfort by keeping sweat from dripping down your face and hands, maintaining better grip and focus. These small additions to your gear can make a significant difference in your comfort and performance on the court.

Specialized Clothing and Gear

For those who take their pickleball seriously or who have specific physical concerns, specialized clothing and gear can provide additional benefits. Compression sleeves and socks are excellent for improving circulation and reducing muscle fatigue. They can also help stabilize muscles and reduce the risk of cramps or strains. For players with joint issues or previous injuries, braces or knee, elbow, or wrist supports can provide the necessary stability to play with confidence. While not everyone will need these specialized items, they can be invaluable for those who do, helping to enhance performance and prevent further injury.

Each piece of clothing and accessory you choose can play a critical role in how comfortably and effectively you play pickleball. From the moisture-wicking properties of your outfit to the protective features of your sunglasses, every item has the potential to enhance your game. As you continue to play and grow in your pickleball journey, take the time to assess your apparel and accessories periodically. Ensure they are meeting your needs and supporting your performance to the fullest. After all, the right gear can be just as important as the right technique in helping you play your best game.

7.5 Maintaining Your Equipment: Care Tips and Recommendations

Taking good care of your pickleball equipment isn't just about prolonging its life; it's about ensuring consistent performance every time you step onto the court. Think of your paddle and balls as trusted companions in your pickleball adventures—keeping them in top condition means they'll always be ready to perform when you are. Let's walk through some essential maintenance tips that will help keep your gear in prime shape, enhancing both your game and the longevity of your equipment.

Routine Cleaning of Paddles and Balls

Keeping your pickleball paddle clean is crucial for maintaining its grip and surface integrity. After each use, remove dirt, sweat, and grime that can accumulate during play by wiping down the paddle face with a soft, damp cloth. If the paddle is particularly dirty, a mild soap solution can be used, but ensure the soap is thoroughly rinsed off to avoid leaving any residue. For the grip, if it becomes slick from sweat or dirt, consider using a specialized grip cleaner or simply replace the grip if it's worn out. This ensures better handling and prevents the build-up of bacteria that can degrade the material over time.

Pickleball balls also require regular cleaning, especially if you play outdoors. Dirt and sand can embed in the holes of the ball, affecting its flight and bounce. Clean the balls by soaking them in a gentle soap solution and then scrubbing lightly with a soft brush to dislodge debris from the holes. Rinse the balls thoroughly and dry them before storing them. This simple cleaning routine can significantly extend the life of your balls and ensure they perform well in your next game.

Storing Equipment Properly

Proper storage of your pickleball equipment is key to preventing premature wear and tear. Store your paddle in a cool, dry place away from direct sunlight, as UV rays can degrade the materials over time, causing them to become brittle and susceptible to cracking. If you're storing multiple paddles, avoid stacking them directly on top of each other without protective padding, as pressure and friction can damage the surfaces. A dedicated racket bag with individual sleeves for each paddle is ideal for protection and ease of transport.

For pickleball balls, ensure they are stored in a temperature-controlled environment. Extreme temperatures can warp the balls, affecting their bounce and durability. Avoid leaving them in your car, especially on hot or cold days, as the temperature inside a vehicle can fluctuate drastically and damage the balls. Using a mesh bag for balls helps keep them together and allows for proper ventilation, preventing moisture build-up, which can lead to mold or softening of the balls.

Regular Inspection for Wear and Tear

Regularly inspecting your equipment can catch potential problems before they affect your game. Check your paddle for any signs of damage, such as cracks on the face or edge, delamination of the surface materials, or a loose grip. Even small cracks can significantly impact the paddle's performance, potentially altering the balance and weight distribution. If you notice any irregularities, it may be time to consider replacing your paddle to ensure optimal performance and safety during play.

Inspect pickleball balls for smoothness and roundness. Over time, balls can become rough and lose their original shape, which can affect how they roll and bounce. If you notice significant wear, such as deep scratches or misshapen form, replace the balls to maintain the quality of your play. Regular inspection is not just about maintenance; it's about ensuring that every game you play is as good as it can be.

Professional Maintenance and Repairs

Sometimes, maintenance requires a professional touch, especially when it comes to re-gripping paddles or repairing damaged edges. If the grip of your paddle has worn down to the point where it affects your hold, consider having it professionally re-gripped. Professional re-gripping ensures that the new grip is applied smoothly and securely, providing you with the best possible handle on your game.

Professional repair services can often restore paddles with minor surface damage or edge wear to good condition, prolonging their life and performance. However, if the core of the paddle is damaged or if the paddle face is severely cracked, replacement might be the only viable option to ensure safety and effectiveness in play.

Maintaining your pickleball equipment might seem like a minor part of the game, but it plays a crucial role in how well you can perform on the court. Regularly cleaning, properly storing, and diligently inspecting your gear ensures that every match is played with the best possible equipment. And when issues do arise, knowing when to seek professional help can make all the difference in extending the life of your beloved pickleball gear. Remember, well-cared-for equipment performs better and keeps you at the top of your game, match after match.

7.6 The Future of Pickleball Equipment: Trends and Innovations

As pickleball continues to captivate and expand its community of players, the innovation in equipment technology is not just keeping pace but often driving the game's evolution. Let's explore some of the most exciting trends that are shaping the future of pickleball equipment, from advanced materials to smart technology, and consider how these developments can enhance your gameplay experience.

Technological Advancements in Paddle Design

The rapid advancement of material science has ushered in a new era for pickleball paddle design. Manufacturers are increasingly experimenting with novel materials that can significantly enhance paddle performance. For instance, the integration of aerospace-grade carbon fiber in paddles is a game-changer. This material offers an exceptional strength-to-weight ratio, providing players with a lightweight paddle that does not compromise on power or durability. Additionally, advancements in 3D printing technology allow for more precise customization of paddle characteristics, catering to individual player needs and preferences. Imagine a paddle tailored exactly to your hand's grip or one optimized for your specific swing style—these possibilities are becoming realities as we speak.

Moreover, the paddle's surface is also seeing innovative treatments and coatings designed to improve ball control and spin. Nano-textured surfaces, for example, create more friction upon contact with the ball, allowing for enhanced spin and precision. This technology can be particularly beneficial for players who rely on strategic placement and spin to outplay their opponents.

Eco-Friendly and Sustainable Practices

Sustainability is becoming a priority in sports equipment manufacturing, and pickleball is no exception. Eco-conscious players will be pleased to know that more companies are now prioritizing green practices in their production processes. This includes using recycled materials for paddle cores and faces, such as recycled carbon fibers, which reduce waste and maintain the high-performance standards expected by competitive players. Additionally, some manufacturers are exploring the use of biodegradable materials for pickleball balls, aiming to reduce the environmental impact once the balls are no longer usable.

The move towards more sustainable practices is good for the environment and resonates with a growing segment of players who value ecological responsibility. By supporting brands that invest in these technologies, you contribute to a more sustainable future while enjoying the benefits of high-quality, innovative equipment.

Smart Equipment

The digital revolution is making its mark on pickleball equipment as well. Smart paddles equipped with embedded sensors are becoming more prevalent. These sensors can track a wide array of data, including shot speed, spin, and hit location. This data can be synced to a smartphone app, providing players with actionable insights into their performance. Imagine finishing a match and immediately reviewing data on your phone that shows your most common hitting zones or how your serve speed varied throughout the game. This technology not only enhances individual practice sessions but can also revolutionize coaching by providing precise, real-time feedback that was previously impossible to capture.

Predictions for Future Equipment Developments

Looking ahead, the integration of advanced materials and smart technologies is expected to continue at an accelerated pace. We might soon see paddles with adjustable balance settings, allowing players to shift the weight distribution based on their in-game needs without changing equipment. Another exciting prospect is the development of adaptive grip technology, where the paddle's grip changes its shape slightly to fit the player's hand better during different types of shots. This could further personalize the playing experience, reducing the risk of injuries and enhancing overall performance.

As these innovations unfold, they promise to enhance how well you play and change how you engage with the sport of pickleball. The future of pickleball equipment looks bright, with technology paving the way for more personalized, effective, and sustainable options that promise to enrich your playing experience. As we look forward to these advancements, it's an exciting time to be part of the pickleball community, where the future is being shaped one swing at a time.

Keeping the Game Alive

As we approach the final chapter, I hope this guide has been valuable to you. Your feedback can make a big difference! By leaving an honest review on Amazon, you'll help other pickleball enthusiasts find this book and improve their game.

Thank you for contributing to our pickleball community. Your support ensures that more players can enjoy and benefit from the sport we love.

Simply click or scan the QR code below to leave your review on Amazon. It only takes a minute, but your impact could last a lifetime.

Chapter Eight
Beyond the Court

8.1 Pickleball for All Ages: Promoting Inter-generational Play

IMAGINE A SPORT WHERE grandparents and grandchildren compete alongside each other, where laughter and cheers break any age barriers—welcome to pickleball, a game truly for all ages. This unique aspect of pickleball isn't just a fun family activity but a profound opportunity to bridge generational gaps, enhance understanding, and strengthen community bonds. Playing pickleball with a diverse age range enriches the experience, providing both younger and older players with fresh perspectives and valuable life lessons.

Benefits of Inter-generational Play

The benefits of inter-generational play in pickleball are vast, ranging from social advantages to psychological and physical perks. For older adults, playing with younger players can bring a sense of youthfulness and vitality, which is crucial for mental health and emotional well-being. It keeps them mentally sharp and physically active, slowing the aging process and improving quality of life. Younger players, on the other hand, gain patience, respect, and empathy by interacting with older generations. They learn strategies and skills honed over a lifetime, gaining not just a game partner but often a mentor. Additionally, this interaction fosters a sense of continuity and tradition, as pickleball skills and stories are passed down through family and community members.

Organizing Mixed-Age Games

Organizing games that are welcoming to all ages involves thoughtful consideration of participants' diverse needs. When planning mixed-age pickleball sessions, it's beneficial to adjust rules and equipment to accommodate everyone. Consider using lighter balls or lower nets for games involving very young children or those with limited mobility. Simplifying scoring for younger players can keep the game engaging while ensuring that the court surface is safe can help prevent falls, particularly for older players who might be at risk.

One effective approach is to organize family-friendly pickleball events or create leagues specifically designed for mixed-age play. These can be casual meet-ups where the emphasis is on fun and learning rather than competition. During such events, encourage older players to share tips and techniques with younger participants, fostering a learning environment that benefits everyone. Additionally, setting up shorter, more frequent matches can keep the game lively and inclusive, preventing fatigue and keeping engagement high across all ages.

Fostering Mentorship and Learning

Establishing a mentorship program within pickleball clubs can be incredibly rewarding. Pairing seasoned players with novices improves skills and forges meaningful relationships that can significantly enhance the club's community spirit. Experienced seniors can mentor junior players, offering insights into pickleball techniques and the nuances of sportsmanship and strategy. This mentorship extends beyond the court, as younger players may share their technology or fitness training knowledge, creating a reciprocal learning environment.

When setting up a mentorship program, it's crucial to facilitate regular interactions and provide structured opportunities for mentors and mentees to practice together. This could be through designated mentorship games, joint participation in tournaments, or even social events that help strengthen the bonds between participants. Such initiatives not only improve play but also build a supportive and interconnected community where members feel valued and invested.

Success Stories

Take, for example, the story of a community center in Florida that initiated a 'Generations United' pickleball program. The program quickly became a community highlight, drawing participants from ages 10 to 80. It was not just about playing pickleball but about sharing life stories, celebrating each win, and learning from every loss. The older participants felt a renewed sense of purpose and connection, while the younger ones developed greater respect and appreciation for the older generations. The program's success has inspired similar initiatives in neighboring communities, proving that pickleball can be more than just a game—it can be a catalyst for community cohesion and inter-generational friendship.

By embracing the inclusive nature of pickleball, you can transform local courts into vibrant hubs of activity where age is just a number, and every game is a chance to learn, laugh, and grow together. Whether through casual games, structured programs, or community events, pickleball offers a unique opportunity to unite generations in a shared love of the game, enriching lives and strengthening community bonds. As you step onto the court, remember that each serve, each volley, is an opportunity not just to play but to connect and build a legacy of inclusivity and mutual respect in the world of pickleball.

8.2 Using Pickleball to Support Charitable Causes

Imagine transforming your passion for pickleball into a powerful force for good in your community. Organizing charity tournaments and clinics not only raises funds for worthy causes but also spreads the joy and benefits of pickleball far beyond the boundaries of regular play. These events can create a lasting impact, fostering a sense of community and generosity among participants. Let's explore how you can harness the spirit of pickleball to support charitable initiatives, providing a playbook for planning, executing, and partnering with local businesses and charities.

Charity Tournaments

The heart of using pickleball for charity lies in organizing tournaments that attract players of all levels, spectators, and sponsors—all united by a common cause. To begin, select a cause that resonates with your community, whether it's health, education, or local disaster relief. Once your cause is chosen, planning your tournament involves several key steps. First, secure a venue that can comfortably accommodate many players and spectators. Local parks or sports centers are often willing to host charity events at a reduced rate or even for free. Next, set a date and start promoting your event well in advance to ensure maximum participation. Utilize social media, local sports clubs, and community centers to spread the word.

When it comes to format, consider a round-robin style, which guarantees that all participants play several games, maximizing engagement and fun. Set a price for entry fees that encourages wide participation while raising significant funds. Remember, additional fundraising can come from raffles, food sales, and donations, so plan these activities into your tournament schedule. On the day of the event, ensure everything runs smoothly by having volunteers in place to manage registrations, scorekeeping, and any unforeseen issues. Finally, celebrate the winners with a simple prize ceremony, emphasizing the real triumph—the collective contribution to a good cause.

Pickleball Clinics for Charity

Another fantastic way to use pickleball for fundraising is to organize clinics where entry fees are donated to charity. These clinics can cater to various skill levels, offering beginners a chance to learn the basics and more advanced players the opportunity to hone their skills under the guidance of experienced coaches. To set up a clinic, partner with local pickleball instructors who are willing to donate their time, or even consider leading a session yourself if you have the requisite skills.

Clinics can be themed around particular skills like serving or strategy, making them appealing to a broad range of players. Promote these events through local sports networks, community centers, and social media. Charge a registration fee that reflects the value of the training while supporting your chosen charitable cause. During the clinic, incorporate fun mini-games and challenges that encourage participation and learning. By the end of the session, participants should feel empowered in their pickleball skills and proud of their contribution to the community.

Engagement with Local Businesses

Partnering with local businesses can significantly amplify the impact of your pickleball charity events. Local sports stores, restaurants, and even non-sports-related businesses can be valuable sponsors, providing funds, products, or services to support the event. In return, offer to feature their logos on event materials such as T-shirts, banners, and social media posts. This not only helps cover the costs associated with organizing the event but also enhances the visibility and reach of your sponsors.

To engage local businesses, prepare a sponsorship proposal that outlines the benefits of their involvement, the visibility they can expect, and the impact of the charitable cause. Be clear about what you need, whether it's financial support, products for raffles, or services like printing or advertising. Building these relationships not only supports your current event but can also lay the foundation for ongoing partnerships in future charity initiatives.

Case Studies of Successful Pickleball-Based Charitable Initiatives

Consider the story of a small town that organized a pickleball tournament to raise funds for its local hospital. The event drew players from across the state and raised significant funds through entry fees, a raffle, and local business sponsorships. The tournament's success helped purchase new medical equipment, demonstrating the profound impact of community-led sports events on local health services.

Another inspiring example comes from a pickleball club that hosted a series of clinics for underprivileged youth, funded by donations from club members and local businesses. The clinics introduced children to a new sport and connected them with mentors who helped foster positive life skills and confidence. The initiative was so successful that it became an annual event, supported by the entire community and contributing to lasting change in the lives of many young participants.

Organizing pickleball events for charity can turn your passion for the sport into a powerful tool for community improvement and social change. Whether through tournaments, clinics, or partnerships with local businesses, each swing, serve, and volley can contribute to a greater cause, leaving a lasting impact both on and off the court.

8.3 Teaching Pickleball: Becoming an Instructor or Coach

If you've fallen in love with pickleball and are passionate about sharing your knowledge, becoming a certified pickleball instructor or coach might be your next great adventure. This role allows you to deepen your skills and pass on your love of the game, helping others improve their play and enjoy pickleball even more. Becoming a certified instructor involves several key steps designed to ensure you are well-prepared to teach effectively and safely.

The first step in this journey is understanding the certification process. Certification for pickleball instructors is managed by several organizations, including the USA Pickleball Association (USAPA), which offers comprehensive training programs. These programs typically include both practical and theoretical components, covering everything from the rules and techniques of pickleball to coaching ethics and player psychology. To start, you'll need to attend a series of workshops and complete a practical coaching examination, which usually involves demonstrating your ability to plan and deliver a pickleball training session. Additionally, you'll need to pass a written test that covers the rules of the game and coaching best practices.

Certification enriches your understanding of the game and provides credibility to your coaching services, reassuring potential clients of your competence and commitment to quality coaching. Furthermore, most official pickleball clubs and courts require instructors to hold a valid certification for insurance and liability reasons, making this an essential step if you're serious about coaching.

Once certified, the qualities you bring to your coaching sessions can significantly impact your effectiveness and the satisfaction of your students. Patience is paramount; remember, everyone progresses at their own pace, and the learning process can be fraught with frustration. Your ability to stay calm and encouraging can make all the difference. Equally important are strong communication skills. Being able to explain techniques and strategies clearly and concisely that adapt to different learning styles will help your students grasp complex concepts more readily. Additionally, a deep understanding of pickleball not just as a sport but as a physical and mental exercise will enable you to provide more holistic coaching that addresses the game's physical and strategic aspects.

Building a client base as a new coach involves a mix of marketing savvy and community engagement. Start by leveraging local sports and community centers, offering introductory pickleball clinics or demonstrations. This helps raise awareness of the sport and showcases your skills and teaching style to potential clients. Consider creating professional business cards and flyers that you can leave with local sports stores, gyms, and community bulletin boards. Additionally, a solid online presence can be incredibly beneficial. Create a professional website or a social media page dedicated to your coaching services, complete with contact information, services offered, student testimonials, and engaging content such as tips, drills, and success stories. Engaging content not only attracts new students but also builds your reputation as an expert in the field.

Lastly, never underestimate the importance of continuing education in your coaching career. The world of pickleball is dynamic, with new techniques, strategies, and equipment constantly emerging. Staying updated through workshops, courses, and other professional development opportunities keeps your skills sharp and ensures that you always offer your students the most current and effective coaching. Many certification bodies offer ongoing training and resources, which can help you stay at the forefront of the sport. Additionally, networking with other coaches and players can provide valuable insights and opportunities for collaborative growth.

By following these steps and continually striving to enhance your coaching skills and knowledge, you can build a rewarding career as a pickleball coach. Not only will you be helping others discover and excel in a sport you love, but you'll also be contributing to the growth and vitality of the pickleball community. Whether you're coaching part-time or looking to build a full-time career, the impact you have on your students' skills and their enjoyment of the game can be profoundly gratifying.

8.4 The Global Impact of Pickleball: Spreading the Game Worldwide

Pickleball's growth from a backyard pastime to an international sensation is a testament to its broad appeal and accessibility. What started in 1965 on Bainbridge Island as a simple family game has exploded into a global phenomenon, captivating players across continents. The reasons behind this rapid expansion are manifold, but fundamentally, it boils down to pickleball's universal appeal. The sport's simple rules and minimal equipment requirements make it accessible to a wide demographic, from children in schoolyards to retirees in community centers. Plus, its social nature and adaptability mean it can be enjoyed almost anywhere, from gymnasiums in the U.S. to beaches in Brazil.

As pickleball has spread globally, it has been fascinating to watch different cultures adopt and adapt the game to fit local traditions and lifestyles. For instance, in India, a country where community and family play significant roles, pickleball has become a popular community sport. Local tournaments often turn into community festivals, with music, food, and a carnival-like atmosphere. Meanwhile, in European countries like Spain and Italy, where sports like tennis already have a strong following, pickleball is played with a competitive edge, and local clubs often offer coaching and competitive leagues. These cultural adaptations not only make the game more relevant to local populations but also enrich the global pickleball community by introducing diverse playing styles and strategies.

On the international stage, pickleball tournaments and competitions are drawing players from around the world, showcasing the sport's competitive spirit and fostering a sense of global community. Events like the Bainbridge Cup and the International Indoor Pickleball Championships have participants from over a dozen countries competing and sharing their love for the game. These tournaments are not just about winning; they're about learning from diverse competitors, experiencing different play styles, and forming international friendships. The camaraderie and excitement at these events are palpable, illustrating how pickleball can bring people together, irrespective of nationality or background.

The role of international organizations in promoting and regulating pickleball cannot be overstated. Groups like the International Federation of Pickleball (IFP) play a crucial role in standardizing rules, organizing world-class events, and ensuring fair play across all member countries. These organizations work tirelessly to foster the growth of pickleball by providing resources, training, and support to develop the sport at the grassroots level in new regions. Their efforts help maintain the integrity of the game while encouraging innovation and inclusivity, ensuring that pickleball remains a beloved sport worldwide.

Seeing how different cultures have embraced pickleball and contributed to its global narrative is inspiring. Whether adapting the game to local traditions, participating in international competitions, or governing the sport through global organizations, the international pickleball community continues to thrive, bringing people together to celebrate sport and camaraderie. As pickleball continues to grow, it will undoubtedly evolve, shaped by the diverse cultures participating, each adding its unique flavor to this dynamic and inclusive sport. As you step onto the court, whether at home or abroad, remember that you are part of a vast and vibrant global community united by a love for the game.

8.5 Documenting Your Pickleball Journey: Tips for Social Media and Blogging

In an era where digital presence is almost as significant as your physical one, documenting your pickleball journey can amplify your experience and even inspire others. Whether you're a seasoned player or just starting, sharing your progress, insights, and memorable moments on social media and blogs can enrich your engagement with the sport and connect you with a broader community of enthusiasts. Let's walk through how you can effectively use social media platforms, start your own pickleball blog or channel, capture compelling photos and videos, and build a vibrant online community centered around your pickleball passion.

Social media platforms like Instagram, Facebook, and YouTube have become vital spaces for athletes of all levels to share their journeys, connect with fans, and engage with a global community. To start, choose platforms that best align with your goals and where your audience is most active. Instagram and Facebook are fantastic for quick updates, sharing photos, and joining pickleball groups. YouTube, on the other hand, is ideal for sharing more in-depth content, such as match highlights, tutorials, and personal vlogs. When posting, consistency is key—aim to share content regularly to keep your audience engaged. Use hashtags such as #pickleball, #pickleballlife, and #pickleballaddict to increase the visibility of your posts and connect with wider audiences.

Engaging with your followers is just as important as the content you post. Respond to comments, ask questions, and participate in discussions to foster a sense of community. Share tips, celebrate your victories, and even your losses—these moments add authenticity to your profile and make your journey relatable. Additionally, collaborating with other pickleball players and influencers can expand your reach and provide fresh content that keeps your audience interested.

Starting a Pickleball Blog

Starting a pickleball blog might be the perfect venture if you're passionate about writing and want to share more detailed content. A blog allows you to dive deeper into topics such as game strategies, equipment reviews, and personal stories. Begin by choosing a blogging platform like WordPress or Blogger that is user-friendly and offers customization options. Your blog should have a clean, navigable design that reflects your personality and makes reading enjoyable.

Content is the heart of your blog, so consider what unique perspective you can offer. Perhaps you can share weekly match analyses, training tips, or interviews with other players. Including a mix of evergreen content, such as "How to Choose a Pickleball Paddle," and more timely posts, like coverage of a recent tournament, will attract a broader audience and keep your blog relevant. To maintain your blog, set a realistic posting schedule that fits your lifestyle and stick to it to keep your readers coming back.

Once you have a steady stream of visitors, you can monetize your blog through various avenues. Consider affiliate marketing, where you can earn commissions on products you recommend. You can also explore sponsorships with pickleball brands or offer paid subscriptions for exclusive content. Advertisements are another avenue, though they should be used sparingly to not detract from the user experience.

Photography and Video Tips

Visual content is crucial in capturing the dynamic action of pickleball and making your social media profiles and blog visually appealing. When taking photos, use a good-quality camera or a smartphone with a high-resolution camera to ensure your images are clear and vibrant. Action shots can be challenging, so use settings that allow a fast shutter speed to capture quick movements without blur. Experiment with different angles and perspectives—overhead shots, close-ups of the paddle and ball, or wide shots that show the entire court.

For videos, whether they are tutorials, match highlights, or vlogs, ensure good lighting and stable footage. A tripod can help stabilize your camera, especially during play. Editing your videos to add music, captions, or highlights can enhance their appeal. Tools like

Adobe Premiere Pro or free alternatives like Shotcut can help you edit your videos to a professional standard.

Building an Online Community

Creating a community around your pickleball journey adds immense value to your online endeavors. Start by encouraging your followers to share their experiences and tips. You could feature guest posts on your blog or collaborate on video challenges. Engaging actively with your audience by asking for their opinions, conducting polls, or creating interactive content can foster a more connected and interactive community.

Participate regularly in online pickleball forums and Facebook groups to share your knowledge and learn from others. Being active in these communities can drive traffic to your social media profiles and blog, helping you grow your audience and establish yourself as a key player in the online pickleball community.

8.6 Future of Pickleball: Predictions and Emerging Trends

As pickleball continues to sweep across playgrounds and sporting complexes around the globe, the horizon is shimmering with innovations and expansions that promise to shape its future. The core of these advancements lies in technological innovations that are gearing up to redefine how pickleball is played, coached, and experienced. Imagine stepping onto a court where your every move is analyzed by wearable technology, providing real-time feedback on your swing accuracy and footwork. Wearable techs, such as smartwatches and performance-tracking sensors embedded in clothing, are on the brink of becoming commonplace in sports training. For pickleball, this could mean more precise coaching tailored to players' individual needs, enhancing their skills more efficiently than ever before.

Augmented reality (AR) is another frontier poised to transform pickleball training. AR systems could allow players to practice against virtual opponents, offering customizable game scenarios that challenge their skills and decision-making under pressure. This technology could also be used to simulate crowded, noisy tournament environments, preparing players for the psychological aspects of competitive play. Furthermore, advancements in equipment materials are expected to produce paddles and balls that are not only more durable but also designed to enhance player performance through improved ergonomic features and dynamic response properties.

Another exciting trend to watch is the expansion of pickleball into new markets. Given the existing interest and infrastructure, countries with racket sports as a strong foothold are prime candidates for pickleball's entry. However, the simplicity and accessibility of pickleball make it an appealing addition to physical education programs in schools worldwide, potentially introducing the sport to millions of students. This grassroots approach not only promotes physical activity but also instills a love for the game from a young age, laying the foundation for future generations of pickleball enthusiasts.

As the sport gains international traction, pickleball strategies and techniques are also evolving. The infusion of athletic talent as more players from varied sports backgrounds enter the arena is set to elevate the level of play and innovation within the game. Strategies that once dominated the courts may give way to more dynamic and varied techniques as players bring different skills and perspectives. This evolution will make the game more exciting and challenging, pushing the boundaries of what can be achieved on the court.

Reflecting on the long-term impact of pickleball on health and society, the benefits extend far beyond the physical. Pickleball's social nature makes it an excellent tool for community building and socialization, contributing to mental and emotional well-being. Its accessibility ensures that it can be enjoyed by individuals of all ages and fitness levels, promoting inclusivity and lifelong engagement in physical activity. Moreover, as communities embrace pickleball, the sport has the potential to become a unifying activity, bridging gaps across age, gender, and socioeconomic status and fostering a culture of health, inclusion, and community spirit.

As we look to the future, the landscape of pickleball appears not only promising but also exhilarating. The integration of cutting-edge technology, the expansion into new territories, and the evolution of game strategies are all set to enrich the sport's profile. Whether you're a seasoned player, a newcomer, or someone interested in the growth of dynamic sports, the future of pickleball offers something exciting on the horizon. As this chapter closes, we turn our attention to the broader implications of these trends, understanding that the journey of pickleball is not just about a sport being played within the confines of a court but about a community and culture that are continuously evolving and expanding, touching lives and shaping futures.

Conclusion

As we reach the end of our shared journey through "Pickleball Made Simple," I hope you feel equipped and inspired to take your pickleball game to new heights. From the foundational skills and rules discussed in the early chapters to the advanced strategies and mental tactics explored later, this guide has been structured to support your mastery of pickleball with a solid grasp of rules, exercises, and flexibility sessions for safety and drill set to improve your skills. We've covered everything you need to know, from selecting the right equipment to understanding the nuances of game tactics.

Physical fitness and proper nutrition play undeniable roles in your performance on the court and your enjoyment of the game. Remember, taking care of your body with the right foods and consistent exercise will keep you playing longer and stronger. We've discussed how injury prevention and physical conditioning are about staying active and enhancing your overall quality of life.

We've also uncovered the mental layers of pickleball, emphasizing that the game is as much about psychological readiness as it is about physical skills. Developing mental toughness and strategic acumen is crucial, especially if you aim to compete at higher levels. Your tactical decisions can profoundly impact your success on the court, and I encourage you to continue nurturing these mental skills.

Pickleball is more than just a sport; it's a community. Throughout this book, we've explored how engaging with pickleball clubs and participating in social events can enrich your life. Whether it's through organizing charity events or simply enjoying a game with friends, pickleball offers numerous opportunities to contribute to and enhance your community.

Selecting and maintaining your equipment is also vital. We've gone through the latest advancements in paddles, balls, and other gear to ensure you can make informed choices that suit your playing style and needs. Remember, the right equipment can be a game-changer.

Beyond the court, pickleball offers endless opportunities for personal growth and community impact. Whether you're interested in coaching, participating in inter-generational play, or using the sport to support charitable causes, there's so much you can do to use pickleball as a force for good.

Now, I encourage you to take everything you've learned and apply it to your pickleball journey. Get out there, practice, and don't forget to engage with the community around you. Whether you play casually or compete seriously, remember that every game is a chance to improve, connect, and have fun.

Continue to seek out new techniques, strategies, and experiences. The world of pickleball is constantly evolving, and staying informed and adaptable will help you enjoy the sport even more as you move forward.

Thank you for choosing this book as your guide. I am grateful for your dedication to improving your game and your enthusiasm for pickleball. Keep sharing your love for the sport, and together, let's keep the spirit of pickleball alive and thriving in communities everywhere.

Here's to many more games, incredible serves, and beautiful friendships on and off the pickleball courts. Keep playing, keep learning, and most importantly, keep enjoying every moment of your pickleball journey.

Appendix A: Detailed Pickleball Rules

Overview

This section provides a concise summary of pickleball rules to give you a quick understanding of how the game is played. For the complete official rules, please visit the USA Pickleball website at usapickleball.org. In case of any discrepancies, the official rules take precedence.

Basic Rules

- **Game Format**: Pickleball can be played as doubles (two players per team) or singles, with doubles being more common. The court size and rules are the same for both formats.

The Serve

- **Arm Motion**: The server's arm must move in an upward arc when hitting the ball.

- **Contact Point**: Paddle contact with the ball must be below waist level, and the paddle head must be below the wrist at the point of contact.

- **Drop Serve**: A drop serve is allowed, where the above restrictions do not apply.

- **Foot Positioning**: At least one foot must be behind the baseline at the time of serving. The server's feet must not touch the court or extend beyond the sidelines or centerline.

- **Direction**: The serve must be made diagonally across the court and land within the opposite diagonal court.

- **Attempts**: Only one serve attempt is allowed per server.

Service Sequence

- **Doubles Play**:
  - Both players on the serving team can serve and score points until a fault is committed, except for the first service sequence of each game.
  - The first serve of each side-out is from the right-hand court.
  - If a point is scored, the server switches sides and serves from the left-hand court.
  - This alternation continues until a fault occurs, and the first server loses the serve.
  - When the first server loses the serve, their partner then serves from their correct side.
  - The second server continues serving until their team commits a fault and loses the serve to the opposing team.
  - After a side-out, the serve goes to the right-hand court, and both players on that team serve and score points until two faults are committed.

- **Singles Play**:
  - The server serves from the right-hand court when their score is even and from the left-hand court when their score is odd.

*Note: At the beginning of each new game, only one partner on the serving team has the opportunity to serve before a fault, after which the serve passes to the receiving team.

Scoring

- **Points**: Only the serving team can score points.
- **Game Points**: Games are typically played to 11 points, with a win by 2 points. Tournament games may go to 15 or 21 points, with a win by 2.

- **Positioning**: When the serving team's score is even, the first server of the game will be in the right-hand court; when the score is odd, they will be in the left-hand court.

Two-Bounce Rule

- **Bounce Requirement**: When the ball is served, the receiving team must let it bounce before returning, and then the serving team must let it bounce before returning. This results in two bounces.

- **Subsequent Play**: After these two bounces, both teams may volley the ball (hit it before it bounces) or play it off a bounce (ground stroke).

- **Purpose**: This rule prevents a serve and volley advantage and extends rallies.

Non-Volley Zone

- **Definition**: The non-volley zone, or "the kitchen," is the area within 7 feet on both sides of the net.

- **Volleying Restrictions**: Volleying is prohibited within this zone to prevent players from executing smashes from too close to the net.

- **Faults**: It is a fault if a player steps into the non-volley zone or on the line while volleying the ball, or if their momentum carries them into the zone after volleying.

Line Calls

- **In Bounds**: A ball contacting any part of a line is considered "in," except for the non-volley zone line on a serve, which is a fault.

Faults

- **Definition**: A fault is any action that stops play due to a rule violation.

- **Consequences**: A fault by the receiving team results in a point for the serving team, while a fault by the serving team results in the loss of serve or a side out.

- **Examples of Faults**:
    - A serve that does not land within the receiving court.
    - The ball hits the net on a serve or return.
    - The ball is volleyed before bouncing on each side.
    - The ball is hit out of bounds.
    - A ball is volleyed from the non-volley zone.
    - The ball bounces twice before being struck.
    - A player or their equipment touches the net or net post during play.
    - Violation of any service rule.
    - The ball strikes a player or their equipment.
    - The ball hits any permanent object before bouncing on the court.

Determining Serving Team

- **Method**: Any fair method, such as a coin flip, can be used to determine which player or team serves first, or chooses side or receive.

For further details and the complete official rules, please visit the USA Pickleball website at usapickleball.org.

Appendix B: 30-Minute Drill Sets

Drill Set 1: Basic Skills and Control

1. Dinking Drill (10 minutes)

- **Objective**: Improve control and accuracy with soft shots.
- **Instructions**:
    - Stand at the kitchen line (non-volley zone line) on one side of the court.
    - With your coach standing on the opposite kitchen line, hit the ball softly so it lands in the non-volley zone.
    - Practice hitting back and forth with your coach, focusing on keeping the ball low and controlled.

2. Groundstroke Drill (10 minutes)

- **Objective**: Improve baseline shots with consistency.
- **Instructions**:
    - Stand at the baseline.
    - Your coach will feed you balls, and you practice hitting groundstrokes (forehand and backhand) back to your coach.
    - Focus on maintaining a smooth, controlled swing and keeping the ball deep in the court.

3. Serve and Return Drill (10 minutes)

- **Objective**: Practice serving accurately and returning serves effectively.
- **Instructions**:
    - Stand behind the baseline (back line of the court).

- Serve the ball diagonally into the opposite service box.
- Your coach will return the serve, and you will practice returning the serve back, aiming for deep shots.
- Switch roles and practice returning serves as well.

Drill Set 2: Net Play and Reflexes

1. Volley Drill (10 minutes)

- **Objective**: Develop quick reflexes and control at the net.
- **Instructions**:
  - Stand close to the net, about 1-2 feet behind the non-volley zone line.
  - Your coach feeds you balls to volley back out of the air (before they bounce).
  - Focus on maintaining a soft grip and controlling the ball's direction and speed.

2. Crosscourt Dink Drill (10 minutes)

- **Objective**: Improve angled shots and control.
- **Instructions**:
  - Stand at the kitchen line on one side of the court.
  - Hit dinks diagonally towards the opposite non-volley zone corner where your coach is positioned.
  - Focus on keeping the ball low and soft, aiming for a sharp angle.

3. Lob and Overhead Drill (10 minutes)

- **Objective**: Develop the ability to execute and defend lobs and overheads.

- **Instructions**:
    - Stand at the baseline and practice hitting high, deep shots (lobs) towards the net.
    - Your coach will hit lobs back to you, and you practice returning them with overhead smashes.
    - Alternate between lobbing and overheads to get comfortable with both.

Drill Set 3: Advanced Techniques and Strategy

1. Third Shot Drop Drill (10 minutes)

- **Objective**: Master the third shot drop to transition from baseline to the net.
- **Instructions**:
    - Serve the ball from behind the baseline.
    - After the coach returns the serve, hit a soft shot (the third shot) so it lands in the opponent's non-volley zone.
    - Focus on making the ball drop softly near the net. Repeat to improve precision.

2. Drive and Drop Drill (10 minutes)

- **Objective**: Combine driving and dropping the ball effectively.
- **Instructions**:
    - Alternate between hitting a powerful drive and a soft drop shot.
    - Your coach feeds balls to you, and you practice alternating these shots.

3. Approach Shot Drill (10 minutes)

- **Objective**: Improve transition from baseline to net.

- **Instructions**:
  - Stand at the baseline and practice approaching the net after hitting a groundstroke.
  - Your coach will feed balls, and you practice hitting an approach shot and moving quickly to the net.

Drill Set 4: Footwork and Movement

1. Footwork Drill (10 minutes)

- **Objective**: Enhance movement and positioning on the court.
- **Instructions**:
  - Practice moving side to side along the baseline, staying low and balanced.
  - Your coach will direct you to move forward to the net and backward to the baseline, simulating the movement to the kitchen line and back.
  - Repeat these movements to improve agility and positioning.

2. Fast Feet Drill (10 minutes)

- **Objective**: Improve quickness and agility.
- **Instructions**:
  - Practice quick side-to-side movements and rapid changes in direction.
  - Use cones or markers set up by your coach to create a footwork pattern to follow.

3. Transition Drill (10 minutes)

- **Objective**: Smooth transitions from baseline to net.

- **Instructions**:

  - Start at the baseline and hit a groundstroke, then move forward quickly to the net.

  - Your coach feeds balls to various locations, and you practice transitioning and responding to each shot.

Drill Set 5: Specialty Shots and Consistency

1. Drop Shot Drill (10 minutes)

- **Objective**: Improve drop shots from the mid-court area.

- **Instructions**:

  - Stand in the middle of the court.

  - Your coach feeds balls to you, and you practice hitting drop shots into the opponent's non-volley zone.

  - Focus on soft, controlled shots that land just over the net.

2. Consistent Serve Drill (10 minutes)

- **Objective**: Practice consistent and accurate serving.

- **Instructions**:

  - Serve repeatedly to different areas of the service box.

  - Your coach will give feedback on placement and technique.

3. Shot Placement Drill (10 minutes)

- **Objective**: Improve accuracy and placement of shots.

- **Instructions**:

  - Your coach sets up targets in various areas of the court.

- Practice hitting forehands, backhands, and volleys to these targets, focusing on precision.

Drill Set 6: Mechanics and Repetition

1. Shadow Swing Drill (10 minutes)

- **Objective**: Perfect swing mechanics without the ball.
- **Instructions**:
  - Stand on the court and visualize hitting the ball.
  - Practice your swing in slow motion for different strokes (forehand, backhand, volley).
  - Focus on the correct grip, stance, and follow-through.

2. Self-Feeding Groundstroke Drill (10 minutes)

- **Objective**: Improve solo practice and ball control.
- **Instructions**:
  - Stand at the baseline with a few balls.
  - Drop a ball in front of you and hit a groundstroke (forehand or backhand) towards a specific target area on the court.
  - Repeat with multiple balls, aiming to maintain a consistent and controlled stroke.

3. Bounce and Hit Drill (10 minutes)

- **Objective**: Improve timing and ball control.
- **Instructions**:
  - Bounce the ball once and hit it, focusing on making clean contact.

- Practice with both forehand and backhand strokes, aiming for different targets on the court

Drill Set 7: Advanced Solo Drills

1. Wall Bounce Drill (10 minutes)

- **Objective**: Enhance ball control and consistency with both forehand and backhand shots.

- **Instructions**:

  - Stand 6-8 feet away from a wall.

  - Hit the ball against the wall using a forehand stroke, allowing it to bounce once before returning with a backhand.

  - Practice varying the speed and direction of your shots to simulate different game situations.

  - Focus on maintaining a controlled swing and keeping the ball low.

  - Repeat for 10 minutes.

2. Shadow Serve and Return Drill (10 minutes)

- **Objective**: Refine serve technique and transition to a ready position.

- **Instructions**:

  - Without a ball, go through the motion of serving, ensuring your stance, grip, and follow-through are correct.

  - After each shadow serve, immediately move into a ready position for an imaginary return.

  - Repeat, alternating between serving to different areas of the court.

3. Bounce and Hit Placement Drill (10 minutes)

- **Objective**: Improve shot placement and accuracy.

- **Instructions**:

    - Stand at the baseline with a set of balls.

    - Drop one ball at a time and hit a forehand or backhand shot towards specific target areas on the court.

    - Aim for deep shots and corner placements, alternating between forehands and backhands.

    - Focus on precision and controlling the ball's trajectory.

Drill Set 8: Advanced Partner Drills

1. Crosscourt Dink Battle (10 minutes)

- **Objective**: Develop control and accuracy during dinking, focusing on angled shots.

- **Instructions**:

    - Both players stand at the kitchen line on opposite sides of the court.

    - Engage in a crosscourt dink rally, aiming to place the ball close to the sideline of the non-volley zone.

    - Focus on varying the speed and spin of your dinks to challenge your partner.

2. Third Shot Drop and Advance (10 minutes)

- **Objective**: Practice the third shot drop and transition to the net.

- **Instructions**:

    - One player serves from the baseline, and the receiver returns a deep shot.

- The server then executes a third shot drop into the opponent's non-volley zone while advancing towards the net.

- The rally continues with both players focusing on controlled drops and net play.

- Alternate roles every few serves to practice both offense and defense.

3. Volley-to-Volley Reaction Drill (10 minutes)

- **Objective**: Improve reflexes and control during fast-paced volleys.

- **Instructions**:

  - Stand at the kitchen line facing your partner.

  - Begin a volley rally, keeping the ball in the air without letting it bounce. Increase the pace gradually to simulate fast exchanges at the net.

  - Focus on softening your grip to absorb the ball's impact and maintaining control during rapid volleys.

Drill Set 9: Advanced Partner Drills

1. Lob and Overhead Defense (10 minutes)

- **Objective**: Master defensive lobs and practice overhead smashes.

- **Instructions**:

  - One player stands at the baseline and the other at the kitchen line.

  - The baseline player initiates by hitting a defensive lob.

  - The player at the net practices moving back quickly to perform an overhead smash.

  - The drill continues with both players alternating roles, focusing on both offensive and defensive strategies.

2. Drive and Reset (10 minutes)

- **Objective**: Combine powerful drives with resetting into a controlled rally.

- **Instructions**:

    - One player stands at the baseline, while the other is at the net.

    - The baseline player hits a powerful drive to the net player, who then practices resetting the shot into a controlled dink or drop.

3. Targeted Serve and Return (10 minutes)

- **Objective**: Enhance serving accuracy and practice strategic returns.

- **Instructions**:

    - Set up targets in different service court areas.

    - One player serves while the other practices returning to the targeted areas.

    - The server aims for specific spots to challenge the returner, who must adjust their position and technique to handle varied serves.

    - Switch roles every few serves to practice both skills.

Appendix C: Exercise Instructions

Planks

Instructions:

1. Start on your hands and knees.

2. Lower your forearms to the ground with elbows directly under your shoulders.

3. Step your feet back to extend your legs, keeping your body in a straight line from head to heels.

4. Engage your core by pulling your belly button towards your spine.

5. Hold this position for 15-30 seconds, gradually increasing the duration as you build strength.

Russian Twists

Instructions:

1. Sit on the floor with your knees bent and feet flat.

2. Lean back slightly to balance on your sit bones, keeping your back straight.

3. Clasp your hands together in front of your chest.

4. Twist your torso to the right, bringing your hands beside your hip.

5. Return to the center and twist to the left.

6. Repeat for 10-15 twists on each side.

With Resistance Bands: Hold the resistance band handles in both hands and anchor the middle under your feet. Perform the twist as described, keeping tension in the band.

Squats

Instructions:

1. Stand with your feet shoulder-width apart, toes slightly turned out.

2. Extend your arms forward for balance.

3. Lower your body by bending your knees and pushing your hips back, as if sitting in a chair.

4. Keep your chest up and your knees in line with your toes.

5. Lower until your thighs are parallel to the ground, then push through your heels to return to standing.

6. Repeat for 10-15 repetitions.

> **With Resistance Bands:** Stand on the resistance band with feet shoulder-width apart, holding the handles at shoulder height. Perform the squat as described, ensuring the band is taut.

Lunges

Instructions:

1. Stand with your feet together and hands on your hips.

2. Step forward with your right foot and lower your body until your right thigh is parallel to the ground and your left knee nearly touches the floor.

3. Push through your right heel to return to standing.

4. Repeat with the left leg.

5. Perform 10-15 repetitions on each side.

> **With Resistance Bands:** Stand on the resistance band with one foot and hold the handles at shoulder height. Perform the lunge as described, keeping tension in the band.

Calf Raises

Instructions:

1. Stand with your feet hip-width apart, holding onto a wall or chair for balance.

2. Slowly rise up onto the balls of your feet, lifting your heels as high as possible.

3. Hold for a moment, then lower your heels back to the ground.

4. Repeat for 15-20 repetitions.

> **With Resistance Bands:** Stand on the resistance band with feet hip-width apart, holding the handles for added resistance. Perform the calf raise as described, ensuring the band is taut.

Bicep Curls

Instructions:

1. Stand with your feet shoulder-width apart, holding a dumbbell in each hand with palms facing forward.

2. Keep your elbows close to your body as you curl the weights up towards your shoulders.

3. Slowly lower the weights back to the starting position.

4. Repeat for 10-15 repetitions.

> **With Resistance Bands:** Stand on the center of a resistance band, holding the handles with palms facing forward. Perform the curl as described, ensuring the band is taut.

Tricep Dips

Instructions:

1. Sit on the edge of a sturdy chair or bench with your hands gripping the edge beside your hips.

2. Walk your feet forward and slide your hips off the chair, supporting your weight with your arms.

3. Lower your body by bending your elbows, keeping them close to your sides.

4. Push through your palms to return to the starting position.

5. Repeat for 10-15 repetitions.

Shoulder Presses

Instructions:

1. Stand or sit with your feet shoulder-width apart, holding a dumbbell in each hand at shoulder height with palms facing forward.

2. Press the weights overhead until your arms are fully extended.

3. Lower the weights back to shoulder height.

4. Repeat for 10-15 repetitions.

> **With Resistance Bands:** Stand on the center of a resistance band, holding the handles at shoulder height. Perform the press as described, ensuring the band is taut.

Note: Always consult a healthcare provider before starting any new exercise program, especially if you have any pre-existing medical conditions. Start with light resistance or no resistance to perfect your form before increasing resistance.

Appendix D: 10-15 Minute Flexibility Session

Warm-Up (2-3 minutes)

1. Light Jogging or Marching in Place

- Duration: 2-3 minutes

- Purpose: Increase heart rate and blood flow to the muscles.

Dynamic Stretches (5-6 minutes)

1. Leg Swings

- Duration: 1 minute (30 seconds per leg)

- Description: Stand next to a wall or hold onto a sturdy object. Swing one leg forward and backward in a controlled manner. Repeat with the other leg.

- Purpose: Loosen up the hips and hamstrings.

2. Arm Circles

- Duration: 1 minute (30 seconds in each direction)

- Description: Extend your arms out to the sides and make small circles, gradually increasing the size. Reverse the direction after 30 seconds.

- Purpose: Warm up the shoulders and upper back.

3. Lunges with a Twist

- Duration: 2 minutes (1 minute per side)

- Description: Step forward into a lunge position, then twist your torso towards the front leg. Return to standing and repeat on the other side.

- Purpose: Engage the hips, legs, and core.

4. Side Shuffles

- Duration: 2 minutes

- Description: Shuffle sideways for about 10-15 feet, then shuffle back. Keep your knees slightly bent and stay on the balls of your feet.

- Purpose: Activate the legs and improve lateral movement.

Static Stretches (3-5 minutes)

1. Standing Quad Stretch

- Duration: 1 minute (30 seconds per leg)

- Description: Stand on one leg, pull the other foot towards your buttocks, and hold. Use a wall or chair for balance if needed.

- Purpose: Stretch the quadriceps.

2. Hamstring Stretch

- Duration: 1 minute (30 seconds per leg)

- Description: Extend one leg forward, keeping it straight, and bend at the waist to reach for your toes. Keep the other leg slightly bent.

- Purpose: Stretch the hamstrings.

3. Chest Stretch

- Duration: 1 minute

- Description: Stand with your feet shoulder-width apart. Clasp your hands behind your back and gently lift your arms.

- Purpose: Open up the chest and shoulders.

4. Calf Stretch

- Duration: 1 minute (30 seconds per leg)

- Description: Place one foot forward and bend the front knee while keeping the back leg straight and heel on the ground.

- Purpose: Stretch the calf muscles.

Cool Down (1-2 minutes)

1. Deep Breathing and Shoulder Rolls

- Duration: 2 minutes

- Description: Stand or sit comfortably. Inhale deeply while rolling your shoulders up towards your ears, then exhale as you roll them back and down.

- Purpose: Relax and release any remaining tension.

This routine combines both dynamic and static stretches, ensuring that your muscles are warmed up before play and properly relaxed afterward. Integrating this session into your daily routine can help improve flexibility, prevent injuries, and enhance your performance on the pickleball court.

Appendix E: Essential Gear for Your First Pickleball Session

Essential Gear

1. **Pickleball Paddle:** The main piece of equipment you'll need to play.
2. **Pickleball Balls:** A set of outdoor pickleball balls (if the court is outdoors) or indoor balls for indoor play.
3. **Athletic Shoes:** Non-marking court shoes or tennis shoes for proper grip and support.
4. **Comfortable Athletic Clothing:** Breathable and flexible clothing suitable for sports activities.
5. **Water Bottle:** Essential for staying hydrated during your session.

Optional Gear

1. **Pickleball Bag:** To carry all your equipment conveniently.
2. **Towel:** Useful for wiping off sweat during breaks.
3. **Hat or Visor:** Provides protection from the sun if you're playing outdoors.
4. **Sunscreen:** To protect your skin from harmful UV rays when playing outside.
5. **Extra Clothing:** For a change after the match, especially if you sweat a lot.

Training Aids (Optional but Helpful)

1. **Cones or Markers:** Useful for setting up drills and practicing specific shots.
2. **Ball Hopper:** Helps in collecting balls easily during practice sessions.
3. **Notebook and Pen:** For jotting down notes or strategies during your training.

Health and Safety

1. **First Aid Kit:** To handle any minor injuries or emergencies.

2. **Snacks:** Quick energy boosts like granola bars or fruit to keep your energy levels up.

Logistics

1. **Court Reservation Confirmation:** Ensure you have a confirmed booking if required.

2. **Map or Directions:** To ensure you can find the court easily and on time.

Additional Considerations

1. **Sunglasses**: Protect your eyes from the sun and enhance visibility.

2. **Sweatbands:** Helps keep sweat out of your eyes and off your hands.

3. **Hand Sanitizer:** Useful for maintaining hygiene, especially after touching shared surfaces.

Make sure you check the weather if you're playing outdoors and adjust your preparations accordingly. Arriving fully prepared will enhance your experience and allow you to focus on enjoying the game. Have a great time on the court!

Glossary

A

Ace: A serve that the receiver cannot touch, winning the point outright.

Angle Serve: A serve where the ball is hit diagonally across the court, typically aiming for the sidelines or corners of the opponent's service box.

Approach Shot: A shot hit while moving toward the net.

Around-the-Post (ATP): A shot that travels outside the net post and lands in the opponent's court.

B

Backhand: A stroke hit on the non-dominant side of the body.

Backspin (or Slice): A shot where the ball rotates backward as it moves, causing it to stay low or slow down after bouncing.

Banger: A player who relies heavily on powerful, hard-hitting shots rather than finesse or strategy.

Baseline: The back boundary line of the court, parallel to the net.

Baseliner: A player who prefers to play from the baseline, often using strong drives and lobs.

Block: A defensive shot usually played close to the net to return a hard-hit ball.

Bounce Serve: A serve where the ball must bounce before being struck. See Drop Serve.

C

Centerline: The line that divides the service area into two equal parts, running from the non-volley zone to the baseline.

Counterattack: A strategic and often aggressive response to an opponent's shot, turning defense into offense by hitting a powerful or well-placed return that puts pressure back on the opponent.

Court: The playing surface, divided into right and left service courts and kitchen.

Crosscourt: A shot hit diagonally across the court.

Cut Shot: A shot with backspin, causing the ball to drop quickly after crossing the net.

D

Dead Ball: A ball that is out of play because of a fault or when the point has been decided.

Dink: A soft shot, usually from the non-volley zone, intended to land in the opponent's non-volley zone.

Doubles: A game format with two players on each side.

Down-the-Line: A shot hit straight along the sideline from one end of the court to the other.

Drive: A powerful, low shot often hit from the baseline after the ball bounces, aimed to keep the opponent on the defensive.

Drop Serve: A serve where the ball is dropped from the hand and hit after it bounces.

Drop Shot: A soft shot designed to land just over the net in the opponent's non-volley zone.

E

Erne: A shot where the player jumps or steps outside the non-volley zone to volley the ball close to the net.

Error: A mistake made during play, resulting in a point for the opponent.

F

Fault: Any action that stops play due to a rule violation.

Feint: A deceptive move or fake action intended to mislead the opponent, causing them to react prematurely or move in the wrong direction, creating an opening for a more effective shot.

Foot Fault: Stepping on or over the baseline on a serve or into the non-volley zone when volleying.

Forehand: A stroke hit on the dominant side of the body.

G

Game Point: The point that, if won, will win the game.

Get It In Serve: The most basic serve focused on simply getting the ball in play.

Grip: The manner in which a player holds the paddle.

H

Half-Volley: A shot where the ball is hit immediately after it bounces.

Hinder: A situation where play is interrupted, usually resulting in a replay of the point.

I

Inside-Out Shot: A shot where a player moves their paddle from the inside of their body to the outside to hit the ball.

J

Jamming: Hitting the ball towards an opponent's body to restrict their swing.

K

Kitchen: The non-volley zone, an area extending 7 feet from the net on both sides, where volleys are not allowed.

L

Lob: A high, arching shot designed to land near the baseline.

Lob Serve: A serve that is hit high and deep into the opponent's court, aiming to land near the baseline.

M

Match: A contest between two teams or individuals, typically best of three or five games.

Match Point: The point that, if won, will win the match.

N

Net: The central barrier dividing the two sides of the court.

Net Player: A player who prefers to play near the net, often using volleys and dinks to control the game.

Non-Volley Zone: The 7-foot area on both sides of the net, also known as the "kitchen," where players cannot volley the ball. See Kitchen.

O

Out: A ball that lands outside the court boundaries.

Overhead: A shot hit over the head, typically used to attack high lobs before they bounce.

P

Paddle: The equipment used to hit the ball, usually made of composite or wooden materials.

Passing Shot: A shot aimed to go past an opponent at the net.

Pickle: A term humorously associated with the origin of the name pickleball.

Pickled: When a player or team loses a game 11-0.

Poach: When a player crosses over to their partner's side to hit a ball.

Point on Serve: A point scored by the serving team during their service turn.

Power Serve: A fast, forceful serve intended to make it difficult for the receiver to return.

Punch: A quick, controlled shot, usually a volley, with minimal backswing and follow-through.

R

Rally: A sequence of back-and-forth shots between players within a point.

Rally Scoring: A scoring system where a point is awarded after every rally, regardless of which team served.

Ready Position: The stance a player takes before receiving the ball, with knees bent and paddle up.

Reset Shot: A soft, controlled shot aimed at the opponent's non-volley zone to slow down the pace of the game and neutralize an aggressive attack, allowing the defending team to regain control.

S

Serve: The shot that starts the point, hit from behind the baseline.

Service Area/Court: The area where the serve must land, divided into left and right halves.

Side Out: When the serving team loses the serve and the other team gains the right to serve.

Sideline: The side boundary lines of the court.

Smash: A powerful overhead shot aimed downward into the opponent's court.

Spin: Rotating the ball to affect its trajectory and bounce.

Singles: A game format with one player on each side.

Soft Game: Play that emphasizes control and placement rather than power, often involving dinks and drop shots.

Stacking: A doubles strategy where both players position themselves on one side of the court before serving or receiving to maintain favorable positioning based on their strengths.

T

Third Shot Drop: A soft shot intended to land in the opponent's kitchen, used to transition to the net.

Tiebreaker: An additional game or points played to determine the winner when the match is tied.

Topspin: A shot where the ball spins forward, causing it to dip.

Transition Zone: The area between the baseline and the non-volley zone. Players often try to avoid playing from this area because it is more challenging to hit consistent shots.

Two-Bounce Rule: After the serve, the ball must bounce once on each side before volleys are allowed.

U

Unforced Error: A mistake made by a player without any external pressure.

V

Volley: A shot hit before the ball bounces on the ground.

Volley Serve: A traditional serve, where the ball is dropped from the hand and hit in the air before it bounces.

W

Winner: A shot that the opponent cannot return, ending the point.

Z

Zone: Refers to different areas of the court, such as the baseline, mid-court, and non-volley zone (kitchen).

References

Rules Summary https://usapickleball.org/what-is-pickleball/official-rules/rules-summary/

A beginners guide to pickleball gear – Tangerine https://tangerinepaddle.com/blogs/guide/a-beginners-guide-to-pickleball-gear

Pickleball Court Dimensions Explained https://www.justpaddles.com/blog/post/pickleball-court-dimensions/

Pickleball Strategy: 13 Tips & Techniques to Win Big https://thepickler.com/pickleball-blog/pickleball-strategy/

7 Pro Tips for a Killer Pickleball Serve https://thepickler.com/pickleball-blog/pickleball-serving-tips/

Pickleheads. (n.d.). *How to play pickleball: The complete beginner's guide.* Pickleheads. https://www.pickleheads.com/guides/how-to-play-pickleball

3 Mistakes to Avoid when Volleying: Pickleball Tips and ... https://www.pickleballuniversity.com/home/3-mistakes-to-avoid-when-volleying-pickleball-tips-and-strategies

3 Keys to Improving Your Pickleball Accuracy https://sarahansburypickleballacademy.com/3-keys-increasing-pickleball-accuracy/

Pickleball Footwork Fundamentals: Moving Like a Pro on ... https://hudefsport.com/blogs/news/pickleball-footwork-fundamentals-moving-like-a-pro-on-the-court

Five Tips for Advanced Pickleball Serving - PCKL https://pckl.com/blogs/pickleball-blog-tips-tricks/five-tips-for-advanced-pickleball-serving

8 Strategies to Improve Your Pickleball Defense https://www.pickleballuniversity.com/home/8-strategies-to-improve-your-pickleball-defense

Offensive and Defensive Strategies in Pickleball https://luxepickleball.com/blogs/news/mastering-the-transition-offensive-and-defensive-strategies-in-pickleball

How To Master The Third Shot Drop In Pickleball And ... https://pickleballkitchen.com/how-to-master-the-third-shot-drop-in-pickleball-and-why-its-so-important/

A 20-Minute Cardio Workout to Boost Your Pickleball Game https://www.silversneakers.com/blog/20-minute-cardio-workout-to-improve-your-pickleball-game/

Strength Training For Racquet Sports https://ksbodyshop.com/services/spst/racquet/

Nutrition for Tennis: Practical Recommendations - PMC https://www.ncbi.nlm.nih.gov/pmc/articles/PMC3761836/

Playing Pickleball? Here Are 5 Tips for Avoiding Injuries https://www.houstonmethodist.org/blog/articles/2022/nov/pickleball-injuries-are-on-the-rise-heres-how-to-avoid-them/

Mental Toughness Training for Athletes https://www.peaksports.com/sports-psychology-blog/mental-toughness-training-athletes/

Sports Visualization Techniques for Athletes https://www.successstartswithin.com/sports-psychology-articles/visualization-for-sports/visualization-techniques-for-athletes/

Sports: Why the World's Best Athletes Use Routines https://www.psychologytoday.com/us/blog/the-power-prime/201207/sports-why-the-worlds-best-athletes-use-routines

5 Winning Strategies for Managing Emotions in Sports https://purposesoulathletics.com/5-winning-strategies-for-managing-emotions-in-sports/

The Benefits of Joining an Adult Sports League http://www.bonsecoursinmotion.com/the-benefits-of-joining-an-adult-sports-league/

Ace Pickleball Club https://www.acepickleballclub.com/

How to Organize \u0026 Run a Sports Tournament in 2024 https://eventpipe.com/blog/how-to-organize-and-run-sports-tournament

Sportsmanship Guide https://usapickleball.org/what-is-pickleball/sportsmanship-guide/

In A Rapidly Growing Sport, Advanced Technology Is ... https://usapickleball.org/news/advanced-technology-is-helping-shape-future-pickleball-paddles/

A Pickleball Paddle Buyer's Guide: How to Pick the Right ... https://pickleballeffect.com/other/a-pickleball-paddle-buyers-guide-how-to-pick-the-right-paddle-for-you/

Indoor vs. Outdoor Pickleballs Explained By Experts https://www.justpaddles.com/blog/post/indoor-vs-outdoor-pickleballs/

Pickleball Gear Maintenance: Prolonging the Life of Your ... https://www.bigdillpickleballcompany.com/blogs/news/pickleball-gear-maintenance-prolonging-the-life-of-your-equipment

Exploring the Enjoyment of the Intergenerational Physical ... https://www.ncbi.nlm.nih.gov/pmc/articles/PMC8293167/

7 Essential Steps for Planning a Sports Event Fundraiser https://bloomerang.co/blog/planning-a-sports-event/

Coach Education & Certification Partners https://usapickleball.org/get-involved/coach-education/

How Pickleball's Momentum Fuels The Racquet Sports ... https://www.forbes.com/sites/jefffromm/2024/03/19/pickleball-as-a-sport-and-a-social-experience-gains-momentum/

Don't Let Pickleball Leave You in a Pickle: Tips for Injury-Free Play. https://www.hommenorthopedics.com/blog/dont-let-pickleball-leave-you-in-a-pickle-tips-for-injury-free-play-39417.html

How do you stay motivated in the sport you play? https://ottawawomensfootball.ca/blogs/community/how-do-you-stay-motivated-in-the-sport-you-play

Experts Discuss Sports Shoes – smod. https://smod.mobi/experts-discuss-sports-shoes/

What is the Difference Between Graphite and Carbon Fiber Paddles -. https://acepickleballpro.com/pickleball-how-to/what-is-the-difference-between-graphite-and-carbon-fiber-paddles/

Learn to Play Pickleball - Oxford Downs in Summerfield, FL. https://betoxford.com/pickleball/how-to-play-pickleball/

USA Pickleball Rulebook - USA Pickleball. https://usapickleball.org/what-is-pickleball/official-rules/?fbclid=IwAR3hZLoqQPjrW51AYN65G9BKmfS5cNeBX0S79xrZpbZy6P6TEfJBha334LA

Printed in Great Britain
by Amazon